Jack Abernathy—The Author

"Catch 'em Alive Jack"

The Life and Adventures of an American Pioneer

BY
JOHN R. ABERNATHY

INTRODUCTION BY KERMIT ROOSEVELT

FOREWORD TO THE BISON BOOKS EDITION BY
Jon T. Coleman

University of Nebraska Press
Lincoln and London

First Nebraska paperback printing: 2006

Library of Congress Cataloging-in-Publication Data
Abernathy, John R., b. 1876.
"Catch 'em alive Jack": the life and adventures of an American
pioneer / John R. Abernathy; introduction by Kermit Roosevelt; foreword to the Bison Books edition by Jon T. Coleman.
p. cm.
Originally published: New York: Association Press, 1936.
ISBN-13: 978-0-8032-5956-0 (pbk.: alk. paper)
ISBN-10: 0-8032-5956-5 (pbk.: alk. paper)
1. Abernathy, John R., b. 1876.   2. Cowboys—West (U.S.)—
Biography.   3. Entertainers—United States—Biography.
4. Wild West shows—United States.   5. Roosevelt, Theodore,
1858–1919. I. Title.
F596.A24   2006
978'.02092—dc22   2005037662

This Bison Books edition follows the original in beginning
chapter 1 on arabic page 9; no material has been omitted.

FOREWORD

Jon T. Coleman

In 1891, at the age of fifteen, Jack Abernathy jammed his hand in the mouth of a large West Texas "loafer" wolf. Instead of losing his fingers, he found his life's work. His fist landed at the very back of the animal's jaw. The wolf tried to bite him, but with his jowls blocked open by the hand, he could exert only a stifled chomp. Unhurt but unable to let go, Abernathy endured the stalemate until a cowboy colleague found him. They extricated the hand, wired the wolf's muzzle shut, and carried the animal home. Thus was born "Catch 'em Alive Jack," the alter ego that would carry Abernathy from Texas to the White House.

Born in Bosque County, Texas, in 1876, Abernathy plowed through a series of western personas during his lifetime. He hired on as a cowboy for the A-K-X Ranch at the age of nine, and by fifteen he was an accomplished "bronc buster," riding the first saddle on "308 wild horses" for the J-A outfit (p. 42). A pianist and fiddler, he entertained the saloon rowdies in Sweetwater, Texas. A hunter, he killed bears and chased wolves with greyhounds. He rushed for land in Oklahoma and fought whiskey runners in Arkansas. He wore the badges of under-sheriff, posse member, deputy marshal, U.S. marshal, and Secret Service agent. He was a homesteader, a rancher, and a wildcat oil driller. He rode a loyal steed called Sam Bass and owned a heroic dog named Catch. Wearing a six shooter, associating with characters like "Blue" Johnson, "Post Oak" Jim, and "Grasshopper" Roberts, and uttering phrases like "I am a goner for keeps" and "Hands up, Keller!," Jack Abernathy could lay claim to an exquisite dime novel identity: he was a singing, gun-

toting cowboy/lawman who busted broncs, settled wilder-
nesses, and drilled gushers. Yet, while manly and romantic
western jobs filled his resume, he chose grasping the lower
jaws of predatory canines as his first talent and principal
contribution to human history. It was a peculiar choice,
and unearthing the reasons for Abernathy's odd presen-
tation of himself is one of the joys of reading his wild,
entertaining, and factually challenged autobiography.

Abernathy captured over a thousand wolves in his lifetime. He sold the animals to "parks, zoos, traveling shows,
and firms which used them for breeding stock" (p. 60). He
also used the animals in his own shows, catching coyotes,
"loafers," and large wolves in one place and transporting
them to parks and prairies where he would stick his hand
in their mouths again in front of an audience. On Christmas Day 1904, Abernathy "entertained" crowds at Lyon's
Park in Texas. The owner of the park, Cecil Lyon, was a
prominent Republican, and he told President Theodore
Roosevelt about Abernathy. The next spring, Roosevelt, a
collection of ranchers, Rough Riders, bankers, and an as-
sortment of cooks, waiters, and manservants gathered at
Big Pasture, Oklahoma, for a hunt with the "bare-handed
wolfer."

Abernathy caught the president's imagination along
with several wolves. After watching him jump from Sam
Bass and secure a coyote "in the usual way," Roosevelt declared, "This beats anything I have ever seen in my life,
and I have seen a good deal!" (p. 115). Abernathy's skill
as a hunter, his knowledge of animals, his physical vigor,
and his plain manners matched Roosevelt's vision of manliness. The wolfer embodied the president's West, a rough
place that tested men. After the 1905 hunt, Abernathy performed for Roosevelt for the next fourteen years, traveling
to Washington DC and New York to dine, box, and regale
the president with colorful western stories.

Abernathy continued this performance in his memoir. His autobiography is a string of adventures with no connective emotional tissue. For instance, he tells the story of "stealing his wife" from her strict guardian, not to explain the bond that compelled the young lovers to defy authority and elope, but to exploit the scene's melodrama. Abernathy's bride is a prop, not a person. Later in the book she appears again—as a corpse. A year after Roosevelt appointed Abernathy the U.S. marshal for the state of Oklahoma, Jessie Pearle Abernathy died, leaving Jack alone to raise their six children. Abernathy dedicates two sentences to this critical turning point in his life. He notes his wife's passing and declares, "I am happy to say that I was able to bring all of them up safely" (p. 141). How did he accomplish this Herculean feat of single parenting? He doesn't say.

The only personal moment in *Catch 'em Alive Jack* comes at the end. Brutally injured in an oil rig accident, Abernathy turns to religion. Unlike his cowboy, wolfing, and marshaling exploits, this incident leads to "a marvellous change in [his] thought and life" (p. 224). None of Abernathy's earlier adventures cause him to alter his behavior or outlook; they are illustrative rather than motivating. Abernathy the cowpuncher, wolf-grabber, and bandit-wrangler occupies a West of affirmation. Each escapade further verifies his manliness and regional authenticity. His personality stays motionless in a whirlwind of stampedes, hunts, shootouts, and trips to Washington. He must have learned from these experiences, reflected on their meaning, felt the pain or joy they inspired, but he keeps his narrative in the ruts of the mythic West until the last pages.

Because of this reticence, Abernathy's autobiography is an incomplete and frustrating account of a human life. Yet, what the book lacks in emotion and honesty, it makes up for as a cultural artifact. It is false in many ways, but it is also instructive. The reader can learn a great deal about how prominent men in turn-of-the-century America wanted and needed regional characters like Jack Abernathy. Through Theodore Roosevelt, Abernathy infiltrated the upper echelons of Eastern society. He met Mark Twain, Andrew Carnegie, Thomas Edison, and John Jacob Aster. The French ambassador Jean A. A. J. Jusserand enjoyed Abernathy's tales, as did the writer O. Henry. Roosevelt introduced Abernathy to Jack London, William F. Cody, Bat Masterson, and Frank James. At White House receptions, Washington dinner parties, and New York City restaurants, the Oklahoma wolfer received an education in playing the part of a westerner. He watched masters of self-creation— Buffalo Bill, London, Masterson, James, and Roosevelt— act the roles of scout, prospector, lawman, outlaw, and great white hunter, and he saw how Eastern audiences reacted to them. Abernathy's memoir records the stories he told and the persona he created to entertain men who had money, fame, and power. He gave them an authentic westerner to rub against; they offered him the spotlight.

A performer all his life, Abernathy enjoyed the spotlight. He passed this compulsion to his children Louis and Temple, who undertook a series of long-distance stunt rides on horseback at the ages of nine and five. They traveled from West Texas to Santa Fe by themselves, and then took off for New York to meet Theodore Roosevelt on his trip home from his big game hunting expedition to Africa. The newspapers chronicled the "Abernathy kids' " exploits. The publicity won them a contract with the Brush Automobile Company to drive a one-cylinder roadster back home. Later, two New York hucksters paid the boys to ride a donkey and an elephant from New York City to Washington DC. The elephant broke down in Philadelphia. The authorities charged the boys with abuse, and Abernathy traveled to Philadelphia to "settle the argument" (p. 185). He tussled

with the police, but after seeing the animal, he agreed to
end the ride. "The elephant," he reports, "really had sore
feet" (p. 185).

A bizarre incident, the elephant stunt hinted at the dark
issue of animal cruelty that surrounded the Abernathys'
limelight. Louis and Temple rode Sam Bass—Jack's favorite
steed—to death during one of their journeys. Also silent
and hidden are the hundreds of coyotes and wolves Abernathy handled. He presents these animals as fearsome
predators. "The wolf," he wrote, "always started to fight by
leaping for my throat" (p. 61). But his success as a wolfer
undercuts his assessment of the animals' viciousness. If the
canines were truly deadly, Abernathy should have lost a
finger or two in the snapping frenzies, yet he claims to have
been bitten only once. How did he stay unscathed?

He credits his fast hands, his physical strength, and his
fighting spirit. The last may have been the most crucial.
Abernathy bullied his quarry, and many of his victims quit
fighting: "When a daring wolf sees a game fight, sometimes he will give up and quit, just as some game men will
quit a fight while others will battle till absolutely forced
to surrender" (p. 61). Given the wolves' social structure,
this reaction makes sense. Relationships of dominance and
submission organize wolf packs. When a dominant animal
confronts a submissive one, the latter often "gives up"—
bowing, cringing, and rolling on its back, exposing its belly
in order to avoid a fight. By grabbing the wolves, wrestling
them to the ground, and sticking his hand in their mouths,
Abernathy cued the animals to submit. They advertised
their subservience to stop the attack; in return, Abernathy
wired their mouths shut and shipped them to zoos and
sideshows.

Jack Abernathy and his wolves stood at the junction of
the Old West and the Odd West, the imagined frontier and
the halls of power. His memoir reveals just how intertwined

American popular entertainment and the American West had become in the opening decades of the twentieth century, and how men as diverse as a West Texas cowboy and a New York patrician used region, gender roles, and animals to create their selves.

CONTENTS

xii CONTENTS

INTRODUCTION

The Wild West has gone never to return. This was, of course, as inevitable as was the passing of the Indian and buffalo before the advance of the settler in his covered wagon. Such has been the undeviating march of circumstances throughout the world.

In the newly opened up frontier, the wild life is the first to vanish. It has been able to exist alongside primitive man with his spear and arrow and trap, for his weapons have been no more than sufficient to keep him supplied with food and clothing. With the advent of the civilized settler, the change has become rapid. Once the wild game has seriously begun to interfere with the settler's crops, he has taken the matter into his own hands and, with the aid of the rifle, he has defended his property and decimated the wild life. With the disappearance of the latter, the entire system of living of the original inhabitant has necessarily changed. A minority has adapted itself to the mode of living of its new neighbors, but the great majority has followed the trail of the vanished game.

For many years, depending in great measure upon the fertility of the land and its adaptability for agriculture and mining, the frontier remains wild and untamed with huge areas under the control of but a few individuals. Then the homesteaders arrive and the great properties are broken up. The vast herds of cattle either disappear altogether or are broken up into small groups. Barbed wire divides the ranges. The amazing advances in the facilities of transportation have of course done much to hasten this meta-morphosis of the frontier. Probably no other single factor has contributed so largely as the automobile.

Jack Abernathy was born and reared in the Old West, and he writes first hand of this vanished phase in the cycle of our country's existence. My father in his *Autobiography* and in *Outdoor Pastimes* has told in no uncertain language of his respect and admiration and friendship for Abernathy. These feelings have been echoed by all with whom he has come in contact and who know him well. The story he tells in the chapters of his book is indeed a valuable contribution to the history of our Nation.

Kermit Roosevelt

PREFACE

My purpose in writing this book is to give the reader a better understanding of American frontier life in the early days of the great West. All that I have related is from actual experience: my whole life from my childhood up was spent in the great plains of our Western country, battling with wild horses, wild cattle, wild beasts—and wild men.

At the age of five I was at home in the saddle; at ten I was a seasoned range cattle rider; and when I reached my teens I took to riding wild horses and had the feeling that I could ride anything. I slept right on the ground, using my saddle for a pillow. My six-shooter was my friend and constant companion.

I have caught over a thousand wolves with my hands, and I suppose I have ridden that many bad horses. During my career as an officer of the Government, I captured hundreds of outlaws single handed and placed seven hundred and eighty-two men in the penitentiary.

Believing, therefore, that the story of my life would not only prove interesting but valuable to the modern reader in understanding a period of our national life which has now passed, I have endeavored to present a faithful and true story in my own language and in my own way.

CHAPTER I

FROM SCOTLAND TO TEXAS

I was born in Bosque County, Texas, January 28, 1876, the second son and fifth and youngest child of Martin Van Buren Abernathy and Kittie (Williams) Thompson Abernathy. The Abernathy family was of Scottish origin. In the intrigues and struggles of the people of Scotland which followed the expulsion of the House of Stuart from the British Throne and its replacement by the House of Hanover, the Abernathys remained loyal to the Stuarts, with the result that, in the time of the great-great-grandfather of Martin Van Buren Abernathy, thirteen men of the family were exiled, and, with their wives and children, came to America in a body, settling in North Carolina. In that colony, this Abernathy clan thrived and increased; and, two generations later, when the thirteen American colonies revolted, the Abernathys, almost to a man, fought for American independence.

My paternal grandfather, Robert Abernathy, was a native of Missouri, born about ten or twelve years before that state was admitted into the Union. His parents were among the very early American pioneers who crossed the Mississippi after the United States bought Louisiana. Reared under pioneer conditions, Robert Abernathy developed the sterling qualities of his time.

He married Miss Patsy Frye, a native of North Carolina, whose family was of Pennsylvania German extraction, and settled in Springfield, Missouri, where he became prominent as a merchant and farmer. The owner of many slaves, he was noted for his kindness and humanity as a master. Indeed, it is a local as well as family tradition that he purchased slaves after they had escaped from the bondage of less considerate owners, whereupon the fugitives voluntarily returned to their new master.

About three years before the outbreak of the war between the states Robert Abernathy migrated with his family to Texas, settling near Waco, where he purchased the McGaha Ranch. Like many other Texas people of his time, Robert Abernathy was strongly opposed to the secession of the Lone Star State from the Union. "Let us give Abraham Lincoln a chance to do the right thing and, if he fails, the people will put him out," he urged. But a majority of the Texas people voted otherwise and the state formally withdrew from the Union. The three sons of Robert Abernathy—John, Forney, and Van— all entered the Confederate Army, though their father actually wept at the seeming dissolution of the great nation of which he had been a loyal citizen from his youth. He lived nearly fifteen years after the return of peace, and rejoiced in the final preservation of the Union.

My father—Martin Van Buren Abernathy (or, as he was more commonly called, "Van")—joined the Waco Rifles, a company of one hundred and thirty picked men, with which he served in the Confederate Army. This service was of the hardest kind. He went through the Vicksburg and Atlanta campaigns, and was severely wounded. A few months before the war ended, he was captured, remaining a pris-

oner until hostilities ceased.   During the latter part
of the great struggle his father had sold the ranch,
accepting payment in Confederate paper money
which, already depreciated, became entirely worthless
when the Government of the Confederacy finally col-
lapsed.   With the family fortune thus reduced almost
to zero, Van Abernathy, veteran of a vanquished
cause, and recently discharged from a military prison,
was thrown upon his own resources at a time when
business conditions were at a low ebb in Texas as well
as elsewhere throughout the South.

During the course of the four-year war, the livestock industry of the Southern States east of the
Mississippi had been all but destroyed.   In Texas,
however, there had been few military operations and
none that could be classed as extensive campaigns.
Meanwhile, Texas had become so isolated from the
rest of the Confederate States that there had been
practically no market for its surplus livestock.   Consequently, cattle and horses had so increased during
those four years that the ranges of the state were
almost crowded.   Van Abernathy, quick to sense the
profitable possibilities of helping to restore the de-
pleted livestock industry of the states east of the
Mississippi from the overstocked ranges of Texas,
went into the business of buying and selling horses
and mules.

The business proved profitable, and within a year
or two Van Abernathy was enabled to take a considerable drove of horses and mules overland to Vicksburg.
Shortly after his arrival there, he met Mrs. Kittie
(Williams) Thompson, the widow of a Confederate
soldier.   It was a case of mutual attraction, and their
marriage followed within a few days.   The bride,

who was remotely of Cherokee Indian descent, belonged to a very respectable and highly esteemed family, her father being a prominent merchant of Vicksburg. She was a woman of high intelligence, strong character, and attractive personality. By a prior marriage, she was the mother of four young sons and two daughters. When, therefore, Van Abernathy returned to Texas from Vicksburg he was a man with family responsibilities. He became a real father to the four step-sons and the two step-daughters, who in later years proved as loyally devoted to him as if they had been his own children.

After living for a year or more at Waco, Van Abernathy and his family settled on a ranch in Bosque County, about thirty-five miles north-east of Waco. This ranch was located on the extreme fringe of the frontier of Western Texas. Herds of buffalo were common only a few miles to the westward, deer were plentiful, bears and panthers were frequently seen, feathered game (from bob-white quail to wild turkeys) were abundant, and wild bees were to be found in the rocky gorges and canyons along the creeks. The surrounding country was broken, hilly, and semi-mountainous. The nearest neighbors lived ten miles from this isolated ranch home. Life under such circumstances was a serious matter, and was rendered trying and dangerous because of frequent raids by the Comanche and Kiowa tribes.

The first building at this new ranch was a single room log structure of fair size. To this was added another room built of lumber from a frontier saw-mill. These two rooms served as bedrooms. Along one side of these rooms another was added, the full length of both. It served as kitchen, dining room, and living-room combined. A porch (or "gallery," as it was more commonly called in Texas) adjoined this kitchen-living-room. Life and living of course were plain and simple, but sincere and honest. From beneath its roof-tree my two half-sisters were given in marriage to two young men who were brothers, and fared forth to build like homes of their own.

The nearest school house was fifteen miles away. A Baptist minister used to visit that school house and preach every month. Eventually he organized a congregation of his communion there. No other religious services were held within a radius of many miles. Mrs. Abernathy was converted there and joined the little congregation. Religion became a part of her everyday life. She lived it, and sought to inculcate in the minds and hearts of her children the spirit of the Divine Master whose precepts and teachings she had accepted and was trying to follow. The influence of her life was such that her children have arisen to call her blessed. The husband and father, though reared in the Presbyterian faith and a member of its communion, joined with his wife in the Baptist fellowship, since there was no congregation of the Presbyterian Church within his reach.

The days of my childhood were distinguished by some definite tendencies which were to characterize and influence my whole life. I was fond of the free and adventurous life of the country. I loved horses and dogs, and was greatly interested in learning the nature and habits of the various wild animals and birds of the neighborhood. I also had a love and natural aptitude for music, both vocal and instrumental, and although my opportunities to develop my musical bent were small, I made the most of them and learned to play the piano and violin and to sing many songs and hymns. The possession of a rather obstinate "will of my own" was manifest occasionally and gave my parents, especially my father, some anxiety and concern.

On one occasion when I refused to adopt the proper formula in asking for things at the breakfast table, my father thought it was his duty to try the rod as a supplement to moral suasion. When, however, after a third punishment, I was still rebellious and began to sing, with great fervour and childish simplicity, one of my favorite religious songs,

> "Jesus paid it all,
> All to Him I owe . . ."

father and the other members of the family concluded that physical punishment had better be abandoned. Although I was stubborn, my disposition (I am told) was neither resentful, revengeful, nor surly, and generally my childhood conduct caused little disturbance in the family circle.

My schooling was limited to less than two weeks, and my religious instruction was received from my mother, who kept a watchful eye over my actions, trying to instil principles of right and wrong.

CHAPTER II

NEW LIFE IN THE CATTLE RANCH COUNTRY

In 1882, my father was thrilled with the stories of opportunity in Western Texas. Bitter Creek, located ten miles south of Sweetwater, county seat of Nolan county, was the place he selected for a cow camp. He bought a ranch, consisting of several sections, from the Franco Land Co. The entire district was free range. The Abernathy cattle were the G-W-A brand. Among the well-known brands in that area were the Circle-S, the H-Triangle, the A-K-X, and the Half-Circle D-T.

Like thousands of others, Van Abernathy loaded all the family belongings into covered wagons and started for Western Texas. There were three wagons, each drawn by two yoke of oxen. There were six saddle horses, each of the three boy riders having two. A herd of three hundred stock cattle was taken along. The riders were Forrest Thompson (my half-brother), Van Junior, and myself.

About six weeks were required to travel the distance from Waco to Sweetwater, where father decided to locate. The ox teams traveled from sixteen to eighteen miles a day. It was about the first of November when the caravan reached Pecan Gap, Brown County, and camped. A big snowstorm overtook the caravan here, and for two days no effort was made to travel. Danger of a stampede forced the cowboys to remain on guard over the herd at night during the storm, each taking his turn in riding around the herd. Despite my youth and size, I took my turn—my first experience of this kind. Guarding a herd from stampeding at night was one of the most dangerous jobs of the plains.

When it started again toward the north-west, the caravan had no trouble crossing the streams, since all of the rivers, except the Brazos, were small. There was but little water in the smaller streams. In fact, there was some trouble in getting water for the cattle. During two days of the time the herd pushed on ahead of the ox teams. The cattle were thirsty and could scent the water, and the cowboys were unable to hold them back. Each time the cattle got ahead of the ox teams the cowboys would let the cows graze till the teams caught up.

Upon our arrival at Sweetwater, my father installed the family in a large tent. The tent was about thirty-two feet long and fourteen feet wide, boarded up inside. The two bedrooms were floored. By Christmas time the family was comfortably housed.

Sweetwater was mostly a town of tents. The western line of permanent settlements in North Texas was in the vicinity of Weatherford, Parker county. Jay Gould was building the Texas and Pacific main line from Fort Worth to El Paso, a distance of more than six hundred miles. Fort Worth was the main cow town, being headquarters for several of the most famous cattle ranches of Western Texas. El Paso, on the border of Texas and Old Mexico, was a strategic point for the terminal of the great Gould railway lines, since it afforded an outlet into a foreign country.

Not since the Civil War has there been opened a

more splendid undeveloped area than the section which was made available following the building of the Texas and Pacific. Located about three hundred miles west of Fort Worth, Sweetwater is but a short distance south of the celebrated South Plains country, noted in earlier days for its herds of buffalo, elk, and deer. There were also panthers, bears, wolves, bob-cats, coyotes, wild turkeys, prairie chickens, and in fact nearly every kind of wild game that lived in mid-continental United States. To add to life's dangers there were rattlesnakes, water moccasins, spreading adders, mountain boomers, tarantulas, centipedes and vinegaroons, or whip-tailed scorpions —the latter being the most dreaded of all.

While the different grading gangs pushed the Texas and Pacific construction across the Pecos Valley that winter, the main quarters for ranchmen, cowboys, outlaws, gamblers, railroad gangs and ruffians who followed the boom, were in Sweetwater. This tented city was temporarily the metropolis of the frontier and was also the shipping point for cattle. Naturally, therefore, it was the meeting place for cow outfits that previously had driven great herds of cattle over the old trails leading from Texas to Indian Territory, Kansas, Colorado, and other points.

California, with its famous gold rush, and Colorado, with its historic Pike's Peak mining boom, had nothing on prosperous Sweetwater in the fall of 1882. Western Texas was a prosperous cow country at that time, the prices of cattle being the highest in frontier history. Ranchmen received gold for their stock and paid off the cowboys largely in gold coin. The entire country was rolling in prosperity in the days of the early eighties.

Among Sweetwater's institutions were the First National Bank, the Delaney Dry Goods Store, the Fritz Grocery, a weekly newspaper, a church, and a school. There were six saloons. Each of the saloons operated big gambling houses with dance-hall girls upstairs. These girls (with lots of paint on them, but not so many clothes) sold liquor to the cowboys and others who visited the resorts. Among the saloons were the Palace Bar, owned by Gillio and Shifflet; the Gilstrap Bar, owned by the sheriff's brother; the W. B. Johnson saloon, and a barrel-beer house owned by a Frenchman whom the cowboys called "Frenchie."

In each of the gambling houses every kind of game of chance known to the gambling world of those days was in operation. The doors were never locked, each resort operating every day and night of the year. Perhaps the largest and most prosperous business of all was the gambling. Great stacks of twenty-dollar gold pieces were placed on the gambling tables. Each player would have four stacks of gold money in front of him. There were about fifty of these tables in some of the large places. It was nothing unusual for a thousand dollars to be "pitched off" in each game played. Dice, roulette, wheel of fortune, poker, and seven-up ran full blast all the time.

About the only law in Nolan County was the rule of the six-shooter. When persons had disputes they settled their quarrels with guns instead of appealing to the courts; for killing a man the slayer would be offered a drink at the bar, while if a man stole a yearling, a mob staged a public hanging.

At this period things began to happen rapidly in

my young life. I was now six years old, and my brother Van, Junior, was ten. We both liked music, and had learned to play simple tunes together. To develop our talent we frequently went to a drug store that sold musical instruments to play the piano, violin, and accordion. Our playing proved popular and drew many customers to the store—mostly cowboys and gamblers. Forrest Thompson, our half-brother, saw our success, and thought there was money in it. He finally made a deal with the proprietor of the Palace Bar, who agreed to hire us to play each night until midnight, paying each of us thirteen dollars a night.

Christmas week in Sweetwater could hardly be described as a time of peace and good will. Every night one or more men were killed in the saloons, but this caused little notice or surprise. This killing mania reached its climax this year one Saturday night about ten o'clock at the Palace Bar, where we were playing.

A feud had long existed between two saloons—the Palace and the Gilstrap. That night Gilstrap and his bartender came over to the Palace. I was at the piano and my brother was playing the fiddle. We heard a noise and somebody shouted: "Look out!" Gillio, who was known as the crack shot of the town, was standing toward the rear of the main bar with his right hand upon the back bar. The first shot fired shattered Gillio's right hand as he reached with his left for a six-shooter. Lunging forward, Gillio fired, hitting Gilstrap. The next moment bullets killed Gillio and his partner Shifflet. When the smoke cleared away, Gilstrap's bartender also was dying. The saloon was crowded at the time

of the battle, and nearly a dozen others were
wounded. A number of the bullets hit the piano
and put an end to our music for that night.

Soon after the fight in the Palace saloon, our
father began to ask questions about all the money
his two young sons had been earning. He had been
at the Bitter Creek ranch all week looking after the
cattle, but, as was his custom, he came home for
the week-end to remain with the family. We had
been giving our earnings to Forrest Thompson, who,
in turn, gave the cash to our mother. Upon learning
the whole truth, mother immediately put a stop to
our playing at the Palace.

Promoters of every kind of entertainment sought
our services, but only once did we appear in public
again at Sweetwater, this being one night at the opera
house, where the Simms Sisters were performing.
(The Simms organization was a traveling show
troupe.) The manager offered our parents eighty-
five dollars a month for each of us if we joined the
troupe, and promised us a musical education. Our
mother not only refused, but she was so angry that
she threatened to scald the manager unless he quit
trying to take her young children away.

Within a week of the pistol battle in the Palace
saloon, Van and I accompanied our father to the
ranch on Bitter Creek, where we began to ride the
range and help care for the herd of three hundred
stock cows. Father was "ailing" at this time as the
result of wounds received during the Civil War.
This illness made him an invalid for nearly five
years, so that he was obliged to entrust to his two
young sons the management of the ranch, as well
as the care of his livery stable in Sweetwater.

During my father's illness my mother kept wishing for the services of Doctor Terrell, a well-known physician who lived at Colorado City, thirty-eight miles west of Sweetwater. In frontier days this was a great distance. The roads were poor and it would have taken an entire day to ride a horse over the prairie to get this doctor. It would be necessary, therefore, to bring him by train. I kept thinking about this, but I said nothing about my plans, even when I heard mother say she was afraid father was not going to live.

Cowboys and others who patronized the livery owned by my father helped me in my plan, though without knowing it. They drank lots of whiskey and often threw the bottles in the mangers at the barn. I collected all of these bottles I could find. These "dead soldiers" brought me eighty cents at the W. B. Johnson saloon next door. With this money I went to the "depot" and paid for a telegram asking Doctor Terrell to come at once by train. Bill Inkman, the operator, wrote the message, since I could neither read nor write. I did not tell my mother about wiring for the doctor till a few minutes before seven o'clock that night. Then I said:

"Mother, there will be another doctor here in a few minutes."

"Who?" she asked.

"Doctor Terrell, the man you prayed for this morning," I replied.

I had enough cash left to pay the cab fare for the doctor upon his arrival, and I left the house immediately to meet the train.

"Doctor Terrell?" I exclaimed, as I saw a man with a medicine case in hand get off the train. The doctor "made himself known," got in the cab, and was soon at the bedside of my sick father. I followed on foot. When I got home, I heard Doctor Terrell saying to my mother,

"If he can stand the medicine, I can relieve him; there is a chance for him to get well."

Two other doctors had pronounced the case a hopeless one. My father did get well, and outlived his wife many years.

CHAPTER III

THE STAMPEDE

When I was seven years old, and we were moving 480 head of cattle to Nolan County, we camped one night at Logan's Gap, Comanche County, Texas. There were about two inches of snow on the ground, and father seemed worried. He gave orders that we would have to stand guard around the herd, saying that this was the kind of night that cattle stampeded. My half-brother, Forrest Thompson, and my own brother, who was eleven, and I, were the riders. Since I was the youngest of the three, my father gave me the choice of hours. I decided to go on duty at four o'clock in the morning. The night was very cold, and when I was called I did hate to get out of that warm bed! But I took my position on duty, riding slowly around the herd for a few times and stopping just west of them. The cattle seemed to be sound asleep and I was also sleepy and cold—when suddenly, like a flash, the whole herd was up and coming toward me. I knew it was a stampede, and my little horse Barlow seemed to realize it, too. He was off like a bullet. Through the mesquite the hoofs of the cattle roared like a cyclone. They were doing all they could, and Barlow was doing all he could. It seemed that they were gaining on us, and I was looking back and hollering and cursing. I knew a few cuss words in Spanish and I used them— but kept going like a blue blaze. Suddenly Barlow put his foot in a hole and almost "turned a cat." I lost my hat, and felt that cold night air cutting me like a knife. I realized I couldn't get to the right or left of the cattle, and I knew if I fell that would be the end. By this time we had traveled perhaps three miles at that break-neck speed, and I had just about given up hope. But I still hung on, and started to sing one of my favorite hymns, "Jesus, Lover of My Soul."

Suddenly my horse broke into a trot, and I looked back and, to my amazement, saw that the cattle had stopped. I slipped out of the saddle, and put my arms as high up on Barlow as I could reach. He, like his rider, was wringing wet and shivering, and I could hear his heart throb as if it would burst. It wouldn't do to let him stand, so I turned him around and started back to the herd, about thirty feet away. They began to "give" and shy from me. Realizing they weren't accustomed to any one on foot, I got back on Barlow and started around the herd in a slow walk, humming the song all the time.

I was shivering from head to foot with the cold.

I had ridden around the cattle two or three times, and was again on the east side of the herd, which was fast lying down once more.

I heard my father's voice calling,

"Oh, Jack."

I answered as loudly as I could, but I was so cold I couldn't yell very loud.

When father dashed up, he said:

"Jack, how come you're here?"

"Barlow brought me here."

"Did you follow this herd?"

"No, father, the herd followed me."

I was jerking all over from cold, and father said:

"Jack, you're freezing to death," and he took off his overcoat and threw it over me.

"Take the coat off, father," I said, "and put it over Barlow: he's the one that's suffering, and he's the one that saved me. If it hadn't been for him, I wouldn't be here."

Father and I then started to build a fire for the night. Presently, along came my two brothers, Van bringing my hat, which I had lost. There we camped.

At daybreak next morning we left the herd and retreated to the chuck wagon four miles away, where my mother and sister made quite a fuss over me after my father had told them the story.

CHAPTER IV

RIDING THE RANGE—ITS LIFE AND CUSTOMS

I now decided to become a rider on the range. (This was in 1885, and I was all of nine.) My first thought was of the great ranches on the Plains, which were located to the north of Sweetwater, and extended over the entire Texas Panhandle to the southern border of Kansas and Colorado, the western boundary being New Mexico. But I was still young enough to want to be near my parents, so that I compromised and got a job as range rider on the A-K-X Ranch, only ten miles south-west of our own.

I had no trouble holding this job because I was already clever with a rope. In those days the law among ranchmen was that "maverick" (unbranded) calves became the property of the ranch outfit whose cowboy was the first to throw a lariat around its neck.

The youngster usually was offered the first throw. There was an extremely generous feeling toward me among the older cowboys, and they showed their interest by seeing to it that I had a fair chance on both work and sports.

Each cowboy who rode the range was equipped with eight riding horses, a saddle, bridle, lariat rope, branding-iron, and a six shooter. I was too small to handle a big .45-calibre heavy-frame gun, and carried a .38 instead.

26

It cost me about one hundred dollars to buy my entire outfit, which included a coat and pants made of California cloth—the best of material—red broadcloth shirt, a broad-brim leather hat, buckskin gloves, fancy riding chaps, and boots that were made to order. A slicker coat for stormy weather I carried behind the saddle. Like that of all other cowboys, my outfit was not complete without a good supply of tobacco and brown cigarette papers, which I carried in my shirt pocket. (I learned to read by studying the printed labels on tobacco sacks.)

My job as a range rider on the A-K-X ranch was to ride all day among the cattle. John Gray, a youth of twenty-four, was my first riding partner. (All range riders went in pairs.) The life was hard but we soon got used to it.

John and I slept separately at night on tarpaulins, which were carried during the day on the chuck wagon. We made up our beds by throwing these "tarps" on the ground, and using Navajo blankets for covers. To keep the centipedes and rattlesnakes from crawling over us we laid the lariat rope around the bedding, in the belief that snakes would not crawl over the lariat; but we soon learned that the most venomous pest of the plains, the vinegaroon, would not stop for a little thing like a rope.

Under the rule of the range, cowboys butchered their own beef for eating. They usually killed a yearling. The rest of the menu consisted of black coffee with sugar, beef and gravy, canned corn, tomatoes, potatoes, and bread without butter. Though the prairies were black with cows, no milk cows were kept there because there was no way to take care of the milk.

Cowboys had ethics and manners that were lived up to, under the rules of the range. No cowboy was permitted to ask for food. The custom was to wait till the cook cried: "Chuckaway." Then there was a wild scramble and rattling of spurs as the cowboys rushed toward the end of the chuck wagon. The first cowboy to reach it got the choice space between spokes in the wagon wheel in which to lay his six-shooter. No one was allowed to eat without taking off his guns. Those who came late had to crawl under the wagon and lay their guns on the coupling pole.

No cowboy was permitted to use vile language or to tell dirty stories at meals. If he did he "had the leggin's put on him," which meant that he was turned over the wagon tongue and whipped with leggings by the entire outfit. If he fought back, his companions held his feet and hands while the leggings were applied. After such a treatment, the cowboy seldom violated the rule a second time. Each offender was especially keen to protect that spot where the leggings fell: it was painful to ride all day afterward.

Except for tin plates and cups, dishes were unknown in cow camps. Knives and forks had iron handles; spoons were tin. As each cowboy appeared at the end of the chuck wagon, he received the entire meal from the cook, who filled the plate and cup he produced. Each cowboy then sat down on the ground and ate.

Dugouts were a part of the accommodations furnished at the headquarters of the ranch. This was before the days of ranch houses in Western Texas. When I began riding for the A-K-X Ranch there

were about 35,000 head of wild cattle owned by this
outfit.   There were more than fifty known brands
of cattle belonging to other outfits using the free
range in the vicinity of Sweetwater and Bitter Creek.
The territory in which these great herds ranged covered an area of land from one hundred and fifty to
two hundred miles in length.   There were possibly
a half-million head in the entire area.

Under the custom of handling the giant herds of
cattle, the range boss was sole dictator and general-
issimo of all activities.   The cowboys would start on
the general cow works from about the first to the
fifteenth of April each spring.   They would ride
forward in one direction, from a quarter to a half-
mile apart, across the range, driving ahead of them
every forked-hoof animal to a distance of about
twenty-five miles, where all of the cattle would be
thrown into a closed herd.   Then all cowboys took
their places surrounding the herd in order to hold
the cows close together.   The range boss would call
upon a representative of each brand to enter the
herd and cut out his own stock.   The outfits would
run their cows to a distance of about a mile, where
two men would hold each brand group.   Sometimes
it required an entire week to separate the cattle of
the many different brands.   Often it was necessary
to move the herds before the work was ended, in
order to obtain fresh grazing for them.

When the cattle of each brand had separated, the
calf branding was started.   Several days were required for this, after which the cattle would be taken
to the respective ranches of the owners.   When the
cattle were separated, the unbranded calves followed
their mothers.   By that means each brand owner

was able to brand his calves while they were away from the others.

"Trimming" the male calves, following each roundup, furnished the cowboys the occasion of the greatest feast of the year. The "trimmings," sometimes as many as ten bushels, were roasted in the fire while the branding was in progress, each cowboy preparing his own. The cook for the outfit also prepared a stew, using every part of the beef, which he cooked in a pot together.

Every cowboy carried a branding iron on his saddle. This iron usually was made from an end-gate rod of a wagon box. The end of the rod was curved and, when the iron was heated, the cowboy wrote the initials or design of the brand. This branding iron became most useful when a cowboy found a maverick not following a branded mother. Under the rule, the cowboy had the right to rope the maverick and brand it—the maverick becoming the property of the outfit placing the brand.

During all of the time that I was riding the range for the A-K-X Ranch, there wasn't a fence of any kind for hundreds of miles in Western Texas. In 1882 an effort was made to build one about ten miles across a tract about twenty miles south-west of Sweet-water. That fence was cut almost every night and a few days later one man was mysteriously shot to death who had something to do with the fence. For years afterward there were numerous cases of line-fence wars between ranchmen and settlers.

Cowboys had always looked forward to "going up the trail," to Ogalalla, Nebraska, on the Union Pacific, or to Dodge City, Kansas, whence the Atchison, Topeka & Santa Fe Railway hauled the great herds to the markets of the East. The Dodge City market had been closed in 1884, when it was superseded for a short time by Englewood, on the Kansas-Indian Territory boundary.

In 1887, at the age of eleven years, I was one of the cowboys selected by the A-K-X Ranch to drive a very large herd of cattle northward over the old trail from Bitter Creek to Englewood, a distance of about five hundred miles. There were about twenty-five cowboys, "horse wranglers," and a cook in the outfit. There were over one hundred head of saddle horses for the cowboys.

From Bitter Creek the trail went northward, crossing Red River near the mouth of the Pease River to the east of Vernon, Texas. The trail led on northward across what is now Tillman County, Oklahoma, passing through the Wichita Mountains near the present-day town of Mountain Park, Kiowa County. None of the country between Vernon, Texas, and the Kansas line was inhabited by white people. The trail passed through the Kiowa, Comanche, Cheyenne, and Arapaho Indian reservations. In order to get through the Indian country, it was necessary to furnish the tribal members with a fat beef every day or two. Some of these Indian tribes could speak but little English, though the majority of them could speak enough to make themselves understood. One old squaw stepped in front of the great herd, saying: "Not without a cow." She got one.

Perhaps the most exciting experience along the entire journey was when the great herd from the A-K-X Ranch reached the south bank of the South Canadian River. The crossing was west of where the stream is intersected by the boundary between the present-day Dewey and Roger Mills Counties, Oklahoma. The river was about a mile wide at the place of the crossing, and the entire bed was covered with water. In fact, rains upstream had placed the river on a rampage. The current was very swift and the water was so deep that the entire herd had to swim part of the distance in crossing. As the cattle plunged into the water it was necessary to force many of them, for they refused to enter the stream. They seemed to realize the danger.

During the most exciting part of the crossing, the entire herd began "milling" (going around and round in closely massed formation) while in the center of the stream. Every cowboy in the outfit was firing his six-shooter and all were yelling at the top of their voices. It seemed as though every cow in the herd was bawling in fear. The din was terrifying, even to seasoned cowboys. The excitement was most intense, and for a time we feared that the entire herd would be drowned and swept down the raging stream. (As it turned out, we lost over a hundred.)

Finally, as a climax to the excitement, George Gardner, herd boss and foreman of the A-K-X, leaped from his horse and did the most daring thing I saw during my days as a cowboy. He walked out on the backs of the cattle, running, cursing, and firing his pistol. He reloaded the pistol several times from his cartridge belt and continued to fire as he urged the other cowboys in the outfit to do likewise. When Gardner reached the north edge of the herd, one old cow took a lead for the north bank and the entire herd followed. Realizing his perilous position as the cattle began to move out of the stream and separate, Gardner knew that, unless he reached his horse quickly, he would either be swept under by the current between the swimming cattle, or be trampled to death as they moved toward the shore. Shouting at the top of his voice to the cowboys and threatening to discharge the entire outfit unless they rescued him, Gardner continued to yell for his horse. On the south bank myself, I urged the other cowboys to give my horse a start, and also to force Gardner's horse into the water so that it would follow me. This they did, and I managed to reach him. Then he and I swam our horses back to the chuck wagon on the south shore, where the cattle had entered the stream.

Gardner then gave orders for the boys to hit the water and follow the herd, which all of them did, except those who helped with the wagon. My horse was led into the stream and went on across. The wagon bed was tied down so that it would not float away. A "spike team" was hooked on ahead and a cowboy rode each horse. Gardner sat in the wagon and held the lines. I was one of four cowboys, each of whom held a wheel as the wagon was floating across. When we reached shallow water, the wagon caused me and the other three at the wheels to get a ducking, each being thrown as the wheels began to turn when they touched bottom. All of us, however, grabbed the bed and were dragged ashore. By good luck, the river bed near the shore was sandy, so that we didn't get stuck.

Immediately after we had crossed the South Canadian, a heavy rain began falling, and did not let up for over eight hours. The thunder and lightning were almost constant during the downpour, causing

great excitement among the cattle as well as the cowboys. Few of the cattle would graze during the storm,
and it was with great difficulty that we held the herd
together.

All that had happened, however, was nothing to
what was to come. Some will call it a miracle; some
just a coincidence. All I know is that it happened,
and that I can never forget it.

As nearly as I can recall, it was about nine o'clock
in the forenoon when the great herd was started
across the river and about two before all were on land
along the north side. I fix the time because the
cowboys were late in getting their "chuckaway" that
day.

While the rain was falling heavily, the herd had
been halted, but the restless ones moved slowly forward. Soon all the cowboys were ordered to the
front.

We learned that a rider from another large herd
which had crossed ahead of ours (and now located
about four miles to the north of the A-K-X herd)
had come to urge the A-K-X outfit to hold back the
herd, fearing trouble. The entire force was somewhat depressed. They were soaked and exhausted,
and it looked as if the terrific storm meant more
trouble. They had donned their yellow slickers, not
to keep off the rain, but because of the cold wind
which followed the downpour.

I was in the rear at the time Gardner gave the
order for the riders to move to the front. As for
me, I only remember that I was so hungry that, as
the old-time cowboys often expressed it, "My stomach
felt like my throat had been cut."

When I had reached the front, pushing my horse

through the herd of cattle, I joined a bunch of about twenty of the riders, standing with the heads of their horses in a circle. All were too miserable to talk— except one, who was cursing fiercely. I soon learned that he was the boss of the other herd on ahead of us. He finally burst out: "I wish that God Almighty, the old bald headed - - - of a - - - - -, would send a bolt of lightning through me."

Almost instantly, it seemed to me, there was a blinding flash of lightning and, simultaneously, a heavy thunder clap, and every horse, including mine, dropped to its knees. When I came out of my daze I thought I had been struck. Then I looked at the foreman of the herd ahead and I noticed he, as well as his horse, was still down upon the ground —and bleeding. There was blood on the top of the man's head—and on the belly of the horse. Both were dead.

Two days elapsed before there was sunshine over the vast herd and the cow outfit. The boys had managed to get their clothes dry and, as the sun shone again, signs of cheerfulness returned as the outfit moved steadily nearer the Kansas line.

At Englewood the cattle were sold, and the men were paid off and discharged. Each of the cowboys received about one hundred and thirty dollars. After deducting enough cash to pay my way home, I had Gardner, the herd boss, send all the rest of my money home to my father. The horses were sold along with the herd. The saddles, blankets, and other belongings of the cowboys were roped and tied securely, then shipped by rail to the ranch headquarters at Sweetwater, Texas.

Upon being paid off in gold and silver, the cow-boys immediately began "taking in the town," which seemed to me the biggest town in the world. John Gray, my first riding companion on the range, looked after me while the cowboys visited the saloons, gam-bling houses, and "resorts." About all I can re-member seeing in Englewood was saloons. When the cowboys took me into a new place, the dance-hall girls called me "baby," and wanted to know what I had done with my bottle.

In recalling the events of going up the trail, I remember that the most pitiful sight to me was the killing of the young calves which were left along the trail. Each morning, for about fifteen minutes, one could hear one pistol shot after another. As each pistol cracked, I knew it was a baby calf being killed. Of course, there was nothing else to do. The calves could not be taken along with the herd. But I refused to take any part in it. I could no more have killed a baby calf than I could a child.

CHAPTER V

RIDING WILD HORSES AND FIGHTING WILD WOLVES

In the spring of 1891 I was fifteen years old. I had become a full-fledged cowboy, and I decided to break away from the guiding hands of my parents on the Bitter Creek Ranch country, leave the A-K-X Ranch entirely, and go to the great South Plains.

The South Plains are located on what is known as the "cap rock," a high prairie plateau. During the day-time in summer the sun is hot but there is a bracing mountain air similar to that in Colorado and New Mexico. The summer nights are cool and delightful. During the fall and winter, blizzards are frequent, and high winds sweep the entire area, causing cattle to drift away for miles toward the south.

On the A-K-X Ranch was an unusually wild broncho, named Bald Pete. When I was ready to leave the A-K-X this outlaw was given to me, on condition that I show I could ride him. No other cowboy on the ranch had offered to ride him, though there were a number who perhaps could have done so. Bald Pete was about fifteen hands high, weighed about eight hundred pounds, and remained thin and bony regardless of how well he was fed. He was white, with whitish eyes, that seemed glazed, though he could see well enough. On one side he carried Bar-O-Dot-Bar, which was known as an outlaw brand supposed to be from Mexico.

I tried to pet Bald Pete but he would not stand kind treatment and would always paw and kick as though he wished to kill me. I never got on this horse that he did not try to pitch me off. The vicious brute could kick my feet out of the stirrups as fast as I could put them in. So, after mounting, I would jerk my feet out of the stirrups, gripping them into his shoulders until he finished pitching. I was thrown a few times before I got onto his tricks. Bald Pete seemed to enjoy being slapped on the side of the head and I often slapped him in getting off. Of all the outlaw horses on the plains, I never saw another just like him.

Leaving Bitter Creek for the South Plains, I decided to measure my strength by riding him to the J-A Ranch. This vast property was owned by the Widow Adair of England. The J-A was part of the famous Goodnight Ranch, one of the biggest of the entire Southwest. I followed the cattle trail from Sweetwater to a frontier store near where Post City, Texas, now stands. I arrived at the town of Matador about the fifth day. Matador is about fifty miles from the J-A headquarters at Goodnight, on the Fort Worth and Denver City Railway.

This was my first trip to the great ranch headquarters, and about all that appealed to me then was the enormous cattle corrals and the row of barracks for the cowboys. There was a dining room large enough for a hundred to sit at the tables.

The best food I ever ate at a ranch headquarters was served at the J-A Ranch. All chuck wagons, cow camps, or ranch headquarters in frontier days were proverbial for their hospitality to visitors. The latchstring was always out. The souls of the frontier settlers were as broad as the brims of their hats. Everybody was welcome to stop and eat or stay for the night. For real friendship, loyalty, and hospitality, the cow camp or ranch headquarters could hardly be surpassed.

All range bosses were plain-spoken. Though they sometimes appeared to be angry in giving orders, that was just their gruff way. Military discipline was necesssary in order to operate a big cow camp successfully and the bosses were obliged to be as firm as military commanders.

I now applied to Mr. Walsh, the ranch boss, for a job riding the range, which paid thirty dollars a month, with board and lodging. After I had worked three or four months, I went to Mr. Walsh and told him that I understood they wanted a man to break wild horses, and that I would like to have the job riding first saddle. (This means riding a bronc until he quits pitching in order to see if he has any bad habits, such as rearing up and falling back on the rider, or falling when pitching.)

"Well, my son," replied Walsh, "you look too young and tender for a bronc-buster. However, if you can stand the test, I will give you a try-out. You will have to ride four horses a day till they quit pitching."

I asked him what the requirements were and he replied, "You will have to saddle your horse, get on him, roll a cigarette, and make it smoke before you leave the saddle."

"That is pretty tough," said I. After thinking a few moments I added, "Where's your horse?"

He replied, "I'll have the boys rope one for you."

Then he called to one of the boys, "Go rope Haystack."

"What in the dickens does he mean by Haystack?" I thought.

Within a few minutes two cowboys came from the corral leading a dark buckskin horse. This horse was perfectly made, well muscled, well built, and a picture to look at. The white in his eyes indicated extreme meanness. He had "rollers" in his nose—that is, he would make a peculiar rolling noise as all bad Spanish horses do. From all these signs I knew I was up against the real thing.

When the boys started to put a saddle on him I said,

"Wait, boys, take my saddle." I jerked it off my horse and handed it to them, saying:

"If this horse kills me or throws me, I want him to do it from my own saddle."

In placing a saddle upon his back, it was necessary to snub his head to the horn of the saddle of another horse. I noticed the boys were winking and talking in low tones to one another while they were doing this. I knelt down and wired the rowels of my spurs, to keep them from turning when I stuck them into the horse's sides if I had to. I got my tobacco sack handy, a cigarette paper singled out, and as I walked around to get onto the horse I said,

"Boys, has this horse any bad tricks?"

"He'll stand up and pitch but you won't know anything about it a few moments after he starts," they replied.

"Well, here goes nothing," said I, using the words that I always used when starting to do anything dangerous. I placed one foot in the stirrup and leaped into the saddle as I shouted, "Pull the bridle off! All I want is a rope."

The bridle was pulled off and the fight was on between the outlaw horse and myself. The horse jumped high and began pitching. As it came down, it landed stiff-legged but I managed to get the cigarette into my mouth, lighted a match, and made two draws, puffing enough smoke to convince the boss that I could qualify so far. The horse kept on pitching. After lighting the cigarette that was required under the test, I had to do some real riding in order to remain in the saddle, but I managed to do it. When it finally quit pitching I was so weak that I could hardly get off that horse. The fight had taken nearly all of my strength and nervous energy. I lay down on the ground to rest, the cigarette still between my teeth.

One of the Chinese cooks came toward me with a tumbler of wine, which I drank. Within a minute or two it so refreshed me that I felt in shape to try again if necessary. But I didn't need to do it. The owner said, "Jack, you've won the grapes." I was hired!

"Well, Mr. Walsh," I said, "I'm not bragging about it. But there is one thing I want to ask you, Why in the devil did you call that horse Haystack? He is a devil on four legs."

"That's easy to explain, Jack. You see that haystack over there fenced in?" (Looking in the direction he pointed, I noticed a stack of hay around a pole about twelve feet high.) "The last man who tried to ride that horse was thrown to the top of that stack. That's why we fenced it, and that's why we call him Haystack."

On the day following the bronc-riding test, the cowboys "came clean" by admitting to me that the horse was an outlaw, and that no one had ever ridden him before, or attempted to conquer him.

As the official bronc-buster for the J-A Ranch, I rode the first saddle on a total of 308 wild horses, at Silverton, the County headquarter seat of Briscoe County, on the South Plains about fifty miles from the J-A. It was my duty to ride two wild horses each morning, and two in the afternoon of each day. On the following day Will Miller, a cowboy known as the "second rider," saddled and rode the broncos. Then they were counted as broken to ride, and were turned over to the other cowboys on the ranch.

About April fifteenth of that spring the cow works started on the J-A Ranch. The riders went south to the Cow House Canyon, a distance of about one hundred and sixty miles from the Goodnight headquarters. The boss of the range said to me:

"I know you like to hunt. I'm going to let you take your hounds as far as Matador. I'll put you in next to the mountains as we journey south. You might get a loafer wolf."

Of course this suggestion interested me greatly. I should explain that within two weeks of my arrival at the J-A headquarters I had traded a Navajo blanket for a pair of poor greyhounds. I fed the dogs well, and while making the rounds through the canyons, I let the dogs chase after coyotes, which were plentiful in that area.

The cowboys rode from a half to three-quarters of a mile apart, with orders to take all forked-hoof animals regardless of brands. On the first day out we did not find any "loafers," but I had a serious accident. My horse hit a cliff and turned a somersault with me when I was after a cow. The fall broke the curb on the bridle and the headstall, and almost broke my back. Indirectly, as you shall see, the fall was even more dangerous.

That night I patched the headstall of my bridle, using the bailing wire twisted together for the curb on the bit. As you may know, the curb on a bit is attached under the horse's chin so that when you pull the reins the curb tightens and helps control the horse.

I was too sore the next morning to wear my six-shooter. I unbuckled it, rolled it in my "suggin" (bedding blankets), and left it in the chuck wagon.

I took my position at the foot of the mountain, and started on the drive. I had gone about a mile when I came up to two large lobo wolves eating at what I thought was a carcass. They looked like Mexican lions and didn't seem a bit frightened at the sight of me. They must have been very hungry. As I watched them closely, I thought to myself,

"They'll kill my two little dogs," but, remembering Mr. Walsh's words, I felt it my duty to tackle them. Knowing that I would be with my dogs at the finish, I said, "Here goes nothing," and spoke to the dogs. They went out like bullets. One of the wolves loped off; the other turned in defiance of me and the dogs. When the first dog hit him, the wolf slashed her across the left side and she fell to the ground—never to get up again. She crawled along, tearing her wounds with her hind feet, with death in her eyes, trying to get to her mate. The wolf and the other dog were both on their hind legs fighting savagely. I never in my life have seen more nerve and loyalty than was displayed that day by my wounded grey-hound. This poor dog continued to try to crawl toward her mate to help him. The other dog managed to hold his own with the monster loafer.

My hair almost stood up as I listened to the exchange of snaps between the dog and wolf. I knew these snaps spelled death to one or the other. I wish I could express my feelings as I watched this great struggle. I had never before owned such faithful dogs, and as they battled there they were facing death—and doing it all for me. I sprang from my saddle, hitting the ground within two feet of the fighting animals. The wolf leaped for my throat, and I struck out with my right hand. This big "loafer" shut his jaws on my hand, but, thanks to my good luck, the hand was far enough inside his mouth to avoid being caught between the long sharp canine teeth. I had learned a great secret! It was that accidental hand thrust back of the canine teeth that taught me how to grapple wolves—and later took me from the cow camp as a guest to the White House.

I gripped the wolf's lower jaw with my right hand, throwing my left hand over his upper jaw. It seemed that I had almost supernatural strength as I hurled this monster to the ground. I landed on top of him, and we resumed the struggle. This being my first adventure in fighting a wolf with my bare hands, I did not realize that the front feet of the loafer would claw me, and that I was facing defeat. Then, with one powerful stroke, the loafer struck my left hand, breaking my grip on the upper jaw.

I was now in a dangerous position. The wolf moved his head, and I felt his canine teeth enter my left forearm, cutting the flesh to the bone. The leaders apparently were severed; blood began streaming from the wound into the wolf's mouth. I began battling for a new hold on him, and managed to get a new grip similar to the one I originally had on the jaw. In this position, as we lay there on the ground, the wounded arm was just over the wolf's mouth. My right hand held his mouth open, allowing nearly every drop of blood from my wounded arm to drain into his mouth. I could hear him gurgle the blood as we lay there and struggled.

My head was almost against the wolf's head. Had he not slashed my forearm when he broke my original hand hold, he possibly would have slashed my jugular vein.

The only way I managed to keep the wolf away from my neck now was by the firm grip which I had with my right hand. I used all the strength I had in holding this grip. It was life or death for me.

While I was struggling with the wolf I heard the beating of a horse's hoofs, and from the regularity of the beats I knew it wasn't a loose horse. The next thing I heard was:

"What in the hell are you doing?"

I recognized my brother's voice. I replied,

"Everything I can do, Van."

Almost instantly I saw a six-shooter placed against the wolf's head and I cried, "Van, don't shoot. Go get the curb off my bridle and we will wire the son-of-a-gun's jaws." You will recall that I had made the curb out of a bailing wire that morning to replace the regular curb broken the day before when my horse had fallen with me. Van brought the curb while I continued to hold the wolf. We wired his jaws so that he could not bite, and also wired his feet.

We then went to the aid of the wounded dog. I cut the strings off my saddle and took several stitches in the wound in the dog's side, Van helping me. The dog was too weak to get up, so we had to leave her. The other dog was not hurt, except for a few minor scratches and cuts on the nose.

I let Van carry the wolf; my arm was paining me badly. We took him to the chuck wagon four miles back. As we passed the "carcass" of the steer at which the wolves had been eating, I noticed the steer rolling its eyes and groaning. I said,

"Van, look! This steer is not dead." Reaching over I pulled Van's six-shooter and fired two shots, killing the steer instantly. When I examined the brand I noticed that the steer's hamstrings were cut. (It is common for a wolf to bring down large cattle this way.)

I tied up my arm with a silk handkerchief which I was wearing around my neck. This stopped the flow of blood, but the wound continued to be very painful. However, I went ahead and covered the territory assigned to both of us in bringing up the herd in the roundup. When we reached Matador Ranch, the wolf was placed on the scales. It weighed 127 pounds; my own weight was 130 pounds.

That night we camped about eighteen miles south from the place where this wolf catch was made. The cowboys made a fuss over the affair and also over me. I went to the range boss and asked him to let Van and me guard together. The boss permitted this and we went on guard duty at three o'clock in the morning. At about five o'clock, after we had finished our guard duty, Van and I began gathering up scraps from the chuck wagon. We got a piece of raw beef and a fresh canteen of water; and, without waiting for breakfast, we rode the eighteen miles to find the wounded dog.

When we got to the dog she was still alive. We placed before her the raw meat but she refused to eat. I then made a dent in the top of my hat, which I filled with water from the canteen. The dog gulped the water down. In a moment she was stricken with a spasm and died.

The loss of this faithful dog was almost like the loss of a brother to both of us. We had learned to depend on her. To cowboys on the range, during stormy weather and lonesome nights, the loss of a faithful dog means something that only those who have had similar experiences can appreciate.

We were about fifty miles away from the nearest doctor. My wounded arm was in a serious condition, and some of the boys feared that blood poison might develop. One of the leaders in my arm had been cut by the wolf's teeth, and it hung out of the flesh about three inches. This worried me for two days, and I knew the wound would not heal without surgery. Since I could not get to a doctor because of the great distance, I decided to have one of the cowboys in the camp cut the leader and dress the wound. I did not think I should have any trouble in securing surgical aid from the boys. There were twenty-seven men in the outfit, some of whom were brave enough to fight a duel. But, among all those brave frontier characters, there wasn't a cowboy in

the camp who had nerve enough to cut the leader
and dress my arm.

Riding up to the headquarters at Matador, I saw
a pair of shears which evidently had been there for
years. (The outfit was using an abandoned sheep
shed for a camp.) I examined the old shears and
found them to be very sharp. When nobody was
looking, I untied the handkerchief from my arm and
used the shears to cut off the leader. I could see
rust on the cut place, but fortunately the sore was
not poisoned. I presume it was only my good health
and luck that made it possible for the wound to
heal without further trouble. To treat the wound
I used axle grease and coal oil.

Chuckaway was called about sundown that night.
Just before the cook made the call, when all the
cowboys were present, I proceeded to "blast out"
the members of the outfit in my own way. I was
angry because all of them had refused to help me.

"All of you would let a man die; you would-be
killers and bad men generally," I said. "You haven't
enough nerve to kill a possum."

I then took the handkerchief off my arm, exposing
the wound, and showing all the cowboys that I had
performed the operation on myself. Then they all
yelled for joy—that it had been done, and that they
wouldn't be called on to do it.

Among the cowboys in the outfit was a youth of
twenty-four, about six feet tall and slender, who was
religiously inclined. The boys teased him by calling him a "sissy" and asking him, "Dear, where is
your face powder?" "Moonfixer" was the nickname
given this youth and, though the cowboys made all

manner of fun of him, he seemed to take it all in good humor.

I took a liking to Moonfixer and we would often be found together away from the other cowboys. One evening we were resting upon the grass, when a disturbance took place at the chuck wagon. One of the boys shouted, "I'll kill you if it is the last act of my life."

"You'll never put your last act into effect," came the reply with an oath.

Those cowboys were known as two of the worst in the outfit when it came to fighting. Each had hold of the barrel of the other's pistol and they were clinched. Other cowboys, who stood within ten feet of the fighters, were afraid to interfere. Almost like lightning, Moonfixer made a few jumps and entered the fight. He seized one of the guns and was reaching for the second, when I ran up and grabbed the pistol which Moonfixer had tried to get. I gave this gun to Moonfixer and the two fighters went at it again with their fists. They spurred each other as they rolled and fought on the ground, till both were exhausted. Moonfixer then stepped up and said,

"Now, boys, aren't you ashamed of yourselves? Get up, wash your faces and be men. Come with me and I will get water for you." Moonfixer talked to the boys like a father, though he was younger than they. The boys made up after the fight, and the onlookers regarded Moonfixer as the hero of the day, and thereafter ceased to make fun of him.

Most of the cowboys were blessed with a keen sense of humor. Some of their jokes were rather rough, it is true; but as a rule the boys were kind-

hearted and generous, even in the midst of their
crude play. Woe be to the fellow who showed re-
sentment, for his share of trouble was sure to be
doubled thereafter; so most of them accepted what
was handed to them with the best grace possible.
Being a tenderfoot was not pleasant at best; but it
was much worse if he did not soon learn to accommodate himself to his circumstances and surroundings.

CHAPTER VI

TWO LUCKY ESCAPES FROM DEATH

Colonel Charles Goodnight was one of the oldest and best-known cattlemen of the high plains of West Texas. During the time I worked on the J-A Ranch, the Colonel became greatly interested in me as a daring bronco buster and because of my horsemanship and my ability to care for cattle. The Colonel granted vacations at full pay to those who showed ability and were loyal to his vast interests. So it was decided that I should be given a week to play before being transferred to the main headquarters at Goodnight. I decided to spend this brief vacation visiting my parents.

My arrival at the home ranch was an opportune one. My father was preparing to do some fencing, and in all plains and prairie regions suitable and durable fence posts were of prime importance. Fortunately, in this instance, the material was near at hand, though very hard to get at. The picturesque Palo Duro Canyon, through which Red River drops from the highlands of the Llano Estacado to the lower plains, easily the most striking feature of its class in the whole of the Plains region, had—and still has—its floor largely covered with a forest of red cedar trees, one of the best post timbers known. Tule Canyon, which is a tributary or branch of the Palo Duro, cut the plain within a few miles of the Abernathy ranch like a great gash about seven hundred feet deep. Plainly, post timber was near at

51

hand and could be had at a merely nominal cost, save for the transportation from the floor of the canyon to the level of the plain above. Since there was no roadway down the precipitous side of the canyon by means of which teams and wagons could get down or up, it would be necessary to rig up a hoist to lift the posts to the brink of the chasm. Accordingly, two large posts were fixed within three or four feet of the edge of the canyon. From these posts to the trunk of a large tree on the canyon floor, sixteen hundred feet distant, a cable was stretched. On this cable a carrier was operated by means of a heavy steel wire which extended back on the level land away from the edge of the canyon, a horse being hitched to the other end of the wire to supply the lifting power. Five or six fence posts were chained to the carrier as the load for each trip.

I joined the crew that operated this post-lifting device, my father, my brother (Van, Junior) and my half-brother (Felix Thompson) being the other members. My father and Felix went to the bottom of the canyon to load the carrier; Van rode the horse that was to pull the wire; and I was assigned to unchain the load and pile the posts away from the edge of the canyon. There was a space of only about three feet between the two upright posts to which the end of the cable was attached and the edge of the cliff where I stood at work. Beneath the edge was a sheer drop of three hundred feet. And in time, it seems, I became careless.

We had pulled about five hundred posts out of the canyon and it was nearly half-past one o'clock in the afternoon of the second day. I was standing near the edge, and beginning to unhook one end of a load of

posts when a gust of wind took my hat off. Without
realizing what I was doing, I grabbed for the hat,
lost my balance, and started to fall over the edge
of the canyon. I grabbed the wire cable above my
head as I started to fall, catching hold with both
hands. My hands were bare and there was nothing
to protect my fingers from being cut by the small
cable. I was gripping the small wire with all my
might, hanging halfway over the edge of the canyon, and my hands were bleeding from the cuts.
Van, Junior, was with his horse some sixteen hundred feet back of where I was hanging, evidently
waiting for a signal. When Van saw my perilous
position he leaped from his horse and came as
quickly as possible to the rescue.

"My God! What will I do?" he shouted. "If I
grab you—you will pull me over the edge of the
canyon."

"Grab a tie rope and tie my foot," I answered.

Van tied my right foot in less than half a minute,
and just in time, for my strength was gone, and I
had to let go. I thought I was a goner, but the rope
which Van tied held me by the leg. My head hit
the rock as I fell over the edge of the wall. I was
unconscious for ten or fifteen minutes.

Van ran to the wagon standing nearby, grabbed a
six-shooter and fired three times—the signal of distress on the range. My father, in company with
Felix, had become uneasy when the carrier ran wild,
returning below, and smashing itself against the tree.
When father heard the distress signal, he started to
come up, followed by Felix. They were compelled
to go a quarter of a mile east before they could find
a place to climb out of the canyon. About fifteen

minutes passed before my father arrived. I did not
know what was taking place. After straddling the
post, father grabbed my other foot and told Van to
tie a lariat to the horn of the saddle on my horse,
then pull me out by the foot. Van did not untie
my right foot from the post until the horse had a
safe hitch. At last I was rescued, to the great relief
of father and Van and also of Felix, who arrived
after the rescue and declared,

"Jack, you will be killed yet."

They gave me a drink of water and soon I was
fully conscious. Van got a handful of axle grease
and wrapped up my cut hands and we all sat down
to rest and think it over.

I had been lying on the ground about an hour
when "Grasshopper" Roberts, a veteran of the Mexican War, and Indian fighter and a natural-born
hunter, drove up. Roberts lived about thirty miles
south of where we were at work. He was much excited when he saw what had happened and exclaimed:

"What are you doing? Are you trying to kill my
boy? I came after him to go bear hunting."

In those days Tule Canyon had plenty of black
bears, deer, wild turkeys, and other game. Grasshopper often had been on bear hunts in Colorado
and other western states. Though I had never been
on a bear hunt with Grasshopper I was ready and
eager to go, for post-hauling no longer appealed to
me. In hunting for bear I used an old-fashioned
double-barrel shotgun, which had plenty of kick
upon the shoulder. It took me only a few minutes
to get the gun, which I usually kept loaded for big
game; and I was on my way with Grasshopper.

Breech-loading guns of any kind were still a

luxury in those days. Few of the cowboys used anything in the way of shotguns except muzzle-loaders.
This type of gun was loaded from a powder horn
with a measure on the end. The powder was poured
down the barrel with paper for wadding. A ramrod, made either of wood or iron, was used to ram
the load. The shot was placed after the powder was
loaded; then some more paper was tamped upon the
shot to hold them close up against the powder. A
hammer and trigger exploded a cap, the fire leading
into the powder chamber.

Each time a muzzle-loader was fired it had to be
reloaded. If the hunter failed to kill, he was likely
to be in danger, especially if his shot only wounded
a bear or buffalo. (A wounded bear is inclined to
charge a hunter.) Sometimes, while trying to re-
load quickly, the hunter would break off the ramrod,
putting the gun out of commission.

We climbed down the rocks and entered Tule
Canyon. Within a few minutes we discovered fresh
bear tracks. Grasshopper asked me if I understood
the distress signal—three long blasts from a horn.
I said I did. Each of us carried such a horn. I
followed the bear tracks to the right and Grasshopper took the trail to the left, in a north-westerly
direction.

I had walked only about two hundred yards when
I saw a black bear coming almost directly toward me.
He was about one hundred yards off and must have
scented me, for he turned and single-footed broad-
side to the right for about fifty steps. Then he
started up the slope. I could have shot him easily,
and do not know why I didn't.

I immediately started after the bear, hoping he

would stop and turn around, so that I could get a
shot. But the bear kept on climbing, making several
turns in going up the slope. Both he and I were
making about the same rate of speed. I was climbing as fast as I could. Then I thought I saw him
go under a rock. When I reached that spot I discovered that he had gone into a cave in the side of
the canyon. By stooping just a little, I found that
I could follow him into the cave. I called and
listened for Grasshopper, but got no reply.

I felt sure the bear was in the cave. Finally I
said to myself, "Here goes nothing—it is me and the
bear," and I started in pursuit, pushing my trusty
muzzle-loader shotgun along with me. The farther
I went inside the cave, the more I had to stoop, and
finally I went down on my hands and knees and
crawling on my stomach, pushing the shotgun ahead
of me. I had advanced about thirty feet into the
cave, when I saw two bright eyes, sparkling in the
darkness like two balls of fire.

I noticed that every time I moved, the eyes would
disappear for an instant, then would show again.
I picked up a rock and pounded on the bottom of
the cave. Each time I made the noise the eyes would
sparkle for a moment, then disappear again. I re-
peated this noise, perhaps a dozen times, and each
time I was placing the shotgun—getting a bead on
the two bright eyes. I realized that if the bear was
hiding his eyes behind a rock, I might be up against
it if I fired and did not kill him. I aimed the gun
about two inches under where I saw the eyes and
pulled the triggers on both barrels. Not being able
to hold the gun tightly against the left shoulder, I

lay there on my stomach, paralyzed for a moment
by the kick from the gun.

The smoke from the heavy load of both barrels
came back into my face and pebbles began falling
from the roof.   I did not move.   At last everything
was still as death.   I decided to crawl ahead to the
point where I had aimed the gun.   I could not fire
the gun again without reloading, so I left it behind
me.   I reached ahead, feeling my way—when suddenly
my right hand touched hot blood.   I had killed the
bear!   Backing out of the cave leaving the gun inside, I hurried to the mouth.   I gave three long
blasts with the horn, hoping to attract the attention of Grasshopper.   Rather to my surprise, he
responded to the signal, and I blew another blast.
Grasshopper answered me again, and I could tell
he was coming toward me.   I could not wait for his
arrival; I was so eager to tell him about the bear,
that I went to meet him.

"We'll have bear meat for supper," I shouted.

"You just think you will," was Grasshopper's
reply.   "A bear is hard to kill."

"That's all right.   This bear is already dead,
for I felt him," I said.

Then I told Grasshopper how I went into the cave
a distance of about one hundred yards (which was
somewhat exaggerated).   He cursed me roundly for
thus risking my life.

When we reached the mouth of the cave, Grasshopper, who was excited, said:

"Do you mean to tell me that you went into that
cave—that there is a dead bear there?"

Then I held up my hand, showing the blood of
the bear and Grasshopper was convinced that I

was telling the truth. He asked me where the gun was and I told him I left it inside the cave.

"You don't regard anything in the way of danger. What if another bear were to come here right now?" he asked.

"I couldn't shoot another bear with that gun if I had it," I replied. "It ruined my left shoulder for today, the way it kicked me."

"Well, I don't know what to do," continued Grasshopper. "If I was to enter the cave and leave you out here to guard without a gun, it would do no good."

I said to him, "You leave me your gun; I can shoot from my right shoulder if necessary."

Both of us decided to enter the cave. We crawled to the dead bear, and after Grasshopper felt the fresh blood, we pulled the carcass about four feet to where there was room to use our knives. The bear weighed about five hundred pounds. We could not begin to lift the carcass, so we skinned and quartered it, and carried the meat out of the cave. We then blew distress signals, which attracted the attention of two other hunters who had a pack mule with them, and they carried the meat out of the canyon, which enabled us to take it to the dugout at my father's new ranch house.

Grasshopper examined the bear's head and front forearms and found that the shot had hit the left forearm and penetrated the top of the head, tearing it open. This produced instant death. The bear, it appears, had been hiding his eyes behind his forearm in the cave, trying to cover up, knowing his eyes could be detected in the dark. (Bears have this instinct.)

"Well," I said to Grasshopper, "this forearm wasn't breastwork enough. From the kick that old gun made, I believe the shot would have broken the rock and killed the bear anyhow."

"If the world knew this," he replied, "you would be branded as crazy."

When Grasshopper said goodbye, he made me promise that I never would go into another cave to kill a bear. We spent the night at the dugout, and we had bear meat for supper and for our meals for several days following.

CHAPTER VII

WOLF CATCHING AS A BUSINESS

At the end of my vacation I returned to Good-night, the main headquarters of the ranch, where for six weeks I resumed work breaking horses. However, the high-jumping, stiff-legged broncos became too tame for me; so, after reading an article in a magazine to the effect that there was a big demand for live wolves, I decided to go into the business of wolf catching. I realized the value of my ability to catch them alive with my hands. Live wolves were worth fifty dollars and coyotes brought five dollars. (This was about December 1, 1891.)

Quitting my job as bronco buster for the J-A outfit, I became a professional wolf hunter. I secured three new dogs and was able to catch any wolf or coyote that jumped up in front of me. Live animals which I caught I sold to parks, zoos, traveling shows, and firms which used them for breeding stock. I used only two of my dogs in catching a wolf or coyote because a third dog was in the way when the time came to make the catch. In the fighting, sometimes a dog would accidentally bite me while trying to bite the wolf.

I have often been amused by the way the dogs acted when nearing the climax in a wolf fight. When the wolf bristled and showed real fight, the dogs frequently would look back to see how closely I was following them. If I was not close, they would not make the attack; but if I was at their heels they would enter the fight at once and in earnest. When I started after a wolf with my bare hands the dogs always got out of the way.

The wolf always started to fight by leaping for my throat. In turn, I always gave him my right hand. Usually I wore a thin glove—the thinner the better for my hand. I wore this glove merely to prevent the sharp cruel canine teeth of the wolf from splitting open the skin on my hand as I thrust it into the back of his mouth. (Wolves' canine teeth are sharp as razors.) However, I have caught many a wolf without a sign of a glove. If I wore gloves, they had to be thin: it required all my strength possible to grip the wolf's jaws, and thick gloves made the job more difficult, especially with the more powerful "loafers."

You don't hurt your hand at all in putting it into a wolf's mouth if you do it as I have described. If you fail, it of course can be extremely dangerous. I do not consider my accomplishment in catching a wild wolf bare-handed any great act of heroism. All big-game hunters must and do possess confidence; but I credit my success in mastering wild "loafers" largely to my determination to win. When I tackled the first wolf with my bare hands, I just decided that I was going to get the wolf, and I did.

In catching more than a thousand wolves alive in this way, I learned from experience that quickness of the eye and physical strength, combined with determination to win, were the prime factors in conquering a wolf. A fighting wolf is like some fighting men. When a daring wolf sees a game fight, sometimes he will give up and quit, just as some game men will quit a fight while others will battle till absolutely forced to surrender.

I was blessed with unusual natural physical strength, which increased as I grew older. During my youth I often "took on" the crack wrestlers who visited our section of Texas. These experiences proved a great help in my battles with the wolves.

I never wanted a monopoly of the wolf-catching feat, and I tried to teach a number of men how to do the trick. It was with no small degree of disappointment, however, that I found all my students were failures in making a catch bare-handed. Nearly every one was able to make the catch up to the point of letting the wolf have his hand. But when the savage animal clamped down on the hand, the student became frightened, fearing the hand was going to be forever ruined. Instead of holding fast to the lower jaw and taking a little harmless pinching, the student quit. Consequently, the wolf then gained the mastery, the student was severely bitten —and I had to catch the wolf.

During the time I caught wolves for a living I lodged at the J-A Ranch headquarters at Goodnight during the winter. I usually caught two wolves in the forenoon and two in the afternoon of each day. I was allowed time for a rest at noon. I used two sets of dogs, and occasionally a change of horses, especially if I had had a long race. On hot days I was particular to save both horses and dogs. I took no chances if the animals gave any signs of being exhausted.

Nearly all of the wolves that I captured while at the Goodnight Ranch headquarters were found in the breaks just before the cap rock. Quitiquay, a town located on the east ridge of Briscoe County, is about six miles from the cap rock. The territory over which I hunted extended from Quitiquay as far south as Matador in the adjoining county—a distance of about fourteen miles. When wolves were not plentiful below the cap rock, I made trips into New Mexico and Colorado, taking horses and dogs along with me. On many occasions I was accompanied by lovers of outdoor sport from the big cities—bankers, doctors, and business men. The guests on these trips went just to see the performance; they never even tried to make a catch.

My father sold the ranch in Briscoe County after living there nearly two years, and the family moved to a farm ten miles south-west of Hillsboro, Hill County, in the famous black-land cotton belt of Texas.

I now decided to quit wolf catching and study music; and accordingly entered the Patterson Institute, Hillsboro, as a piano student. Professor J. B. Taliaferro was the musical director at the Institute. He was a really skilled musician, having played before Paderewski, and before some of the crowned heads of Europe.

I lived at a private boarding house. In the meantime I had learned to read and write and to solve problems in arithmetic. This much education had been picked up in my business dealings while following ranch life on the frontier. Whatever else I knew of life had been received solely in the school of hard knocks and experience. This was in 1893; I was then seventeen years old.

My decision to quit the rugged, rough-and-tumble

outdoor life of cowboy and catcher of wolves and to seek a musical education was possibly an unprecedented incident in the life of such a youth as I was.   I realized in a way that, throughout the Plains region, and even far beyond, I had become known as a wolf catcher.   To that extent—for the cowboy world was my world—I possibly realized that I had accomplished in this new line of sport something out of the ordinary.   The men of my world gave me ungrudging honor because of the skill I had thus attained, for they revelled in the achievements of hardy, rugged, outdoor life.   Thus far there had been no disappointments or failures in my life to cause me to turn my back upon these fellow plainsmen who were so generous in their admiration and praise of my skill and attainments.   I only know that some strange urge within seemed to call me suddenly to break with my past and seek a new world to develop a talent that from my earliest childhood had been a source of great pleasure and satisfaction. I had never even seen a college, to say nothing of entering its portals, and I had very hazy ideas, if any, of the larger cultural life that might lie beyond. Undoubtedly, the fact that my parents had recently moved to Hillsboro had more to do with guiding my footsteps thither than any other influence.

CHAPTER VIII

I STEAL A GIRL

Hillsboro, county seat of Hill county, Texas, was a city of about 14,000 population at the time I was enrolled as a piano student at Patterson Institute. It is on the main line of Missouri, Kansas and Texas Railway, being about half-way between Fort Worth and Waco, in a most prosperous community surrounded by its black-land cotton farms. However, the town seemed like a slow, sleepy place to me after my years on the frontier.

One day soon after entering the Institute I discovered something that I hadn't known existed. I had been writing musical scales on the blackboard, and had made a number of errors. A young girl teacher, who was watching the work of the pupils, came forward and corrected my work.

As I watched her, for the first time in my life I was thrilled with thoughts of love. "She is the sweetest girl I ever saw," I said to myself. She had gray eyes and reddish-black hair braided down her back. I did not then know her name and she did not speak a word to me while making the blackboard corrections. Later in the day, however, I learned that she was Miss Jessie Pearl Jordan, niece of Professor Taliaferro. It was just a case of love at first sight for both of us. I was unable to do much courting except while taking music lessons, but that was opportunity enough.

Pearlie and her sister Lulu were orphans. Their

mother had died when Pearlie was nine. Both of the children from early youth had been tutored in the home of Professor Taliaferro's mother. Since he had helped rear and educate the girls, he naturally took a close interest in their affairs.

I knew that trouble was brewing for me, but I made up my mind to win the girl. With as much determination as I had displayed in catching a wild wolf alive or in shooting a bear inside a cave, I started a fight to a finish. I lost all interest in my studies, deciding that one music teacher in the family would be enough.

Professor Taliaferro soon resigned from the Patterson Institute, and went to Galveston to become Director of Ball College. Up till this time he was entirely ignorant of the love affair, or he would not have urged me to go along to Galveston to continue my studies. Naturally I was easily persuaded to go along, and made no objection to the proposal that I should live with the Professor's family.

Pearlie and I became secretly engaged soon after moving to Galveston. We saw no hope of winning the Professor's consent to our marriage, so we decided to elope. When the Professor finally learned of our love, he started to make trouble; but my fighting spirit arose to support me in my efforts to stage my biggest catch. However, I realized that I had a real battle ahead of me.

From the days of my childhood I had always confided in my parents when I was in trouble. They were my best friends, I knew. I decided now to go to the family home in Hill County and talk over my love affair. This was in 1894. I was eighteen and Pearlie was nine months younger. When I got to Hillsboro, my father approved my plans, and gave me two hundred dollars. We decided that I should return to Galveston, which I did three days later. On the way back my whole thought was how to capture the prize and outwit the Professor.

I learned the schedule of every north-bound train out of Houston. Then I went back to Professor Taliaferro's home. Pearlie was at the piano. I had been talking to her only a few minutes when her grandmother entered, but I had had time to confide my plans. I immediately went to my room, but slipped out later to the Court House to get a marriage license. To my surprise I learned that orders had been given to refuse the issuance of a license permitting the marriage of Jessie Pearlie Jordan. This was a great blow to me. However, I made up my mind to win the girl if I had to do some real fighting, so I went to a gun store and bought more cartridges for my .38 calibre six-shooter. (I carried this pistol under my left arm.) To me, at that period of my life, arming myself to accomplish my purpose was both logical and just. Defiance of the law never entered my mind. All my life I had seen contests settled that way, and I was following the custom I knew.

Our plan was to leave by boat, buggy, or train. I engaged a boat at the dock to go to Texas City, across the bay from Galveston, for eight o'clock that night. I deposited a dollar for the boat, which was reserved for my use. I also arranged for a two-horse team to be hitched up at the livery stable; also for a call carriage to be at the corner of N Street, about a block away from the Taliaferro home, that night at seven-thirty. I went to still another place and en-

gaged a call carriage, to be at 0½ Street, next door
to the Professor's house. Then I returned to my
room.

Upon entering the Taliaferro home, I sat down
and wrote a long letter to Pearlie, who was in another
part of the house. I gave her directions for carrying out our plans for an elopement that night.

"Two minutes after I leave the house tonight,"
I wrote her, "please go out the back door and climb
through a hole in the fence into Mrs. Dillon's yard.
Meet me at the front gate. I am giving you a letter
to leave on the dining table for your grandmother."

In my letter to the grandmother, I assured her
that she need not feel uneasy about Pearlie—that
we would get married at once, and that I would
take good care of her. I also told her about being
refused a marriage license by the clerk, who told me
that the Professor had demanded this, for he didn't
want me to marry his niece.

I gave the letters to Pearlie, then went down the
back way and kicked two palings off the fence, making
an opening big enough for a person to crawl through.
I then came back up to my room, passing Pearlie. As
I passed her, I said, "Carry out the instructions to
the letter." I returned to my room and laid out the
clothes I wanted to wear. I cleaned my six-shooter,
oiling the gun so that it would work to perfection.

By this time the Professor had come up to my
room, acting very friendly.

"I didn't expect you back so soon," he said.

"You won't expect me to leave so soon, either,"
I thought to myself.

Just as they were leaving the dinner table that
evening the Professor said,

"Get ready; I want you to go to choir practice with me tonight."

"I'd like to be excused, Professor, I don't feel very well," I replied.

"It doesn't make any difference. I have told all the singers you would be there tonight, and you must go."

"Very well," I said, knowing this would furnish a good excuse for me to put on my best clothes. I went to my room, dressed hurriedly, and left the house in company with the Professor.

We walked together about five or six blocks. My brain was in a whirl, trying to figure out just how I could catch the north-bound train at eight o'clock without the Professor finding it out. In my desperation, I tried to make myself sick by swallowing the end of my cigarette and was so successful that the Professor became convinced that I really was sick and said,

"Here, you catch this street car coming now and go back to the house. I will excuse myself from choir practice and be with you inside of thirty minutes."

I caught the car and, upon reaching the house, ran up to my room, grabbed my gun and personal belongings, and then made my exit through the front door, my sickness forgotten.

Pearlie knew of my sudden return and joined me in front of the Dillon house, where the carriage was waiting.

"Do you think we can make the eight o'clock train?" I asked the driver.

"Sure," he said. He whipped the horses and we raced at full speed to the depot.

Old Mrs. Taliaferro screamed when she knew that Pearlie had left the house. I knew then that she would immediately telephone the Professor, so there was no time to lose in getting away with the girl.

"If they get anybody, Pearlie, it will be me, so you need not worry," I said, as we boarded the train; "but if they do get me and I live, we will be married before it is all over."

You can imagine how relieved I felt when I heard the station gong sound the signal for the train to move out north. I stood on the platform watching in every direction, but no one tried to stop us.

I got off at each small town between Galveston and Houston to see if I could hear anything. I felt sure that officers along the route would be asked to arrest us. But there were no signs of trouble till we reached Houston. I followed the conductor off the train as it came to a stop. Then two men approached the conductor, one of them saying jokingly,

"Conductor, you have a couple of thieves on that train."

"What?" replied the conductor.

The officer continued,

"No. It's a couple of school kids running away."

"Yes, there is such a couple in the last coach back yonder," replied the conductor.

After hearing this I ran to the back coach as quickly as possible. I said to Pearlie,

"Follow me!" and we went to the back door of the coach.

"Boss, you will have to go out the other way," said the Negro porter, when I told him we wanted to get off.

Quicker than I ever drew a gun in my life before,

I took a drop on this Negro, pointing the pistol into his face, and saying,

"Open that door and open it quick!" Needless to say, the door was opened. Again my frontier life in cattle camps caused me to violate a state law without realizing I was doing so. I was following a custom familiar to me from childhood.

We stepped off on the dark side of the train and as I looked back through the window of the coach I chuckled to myself. I could see the sheriff and deputy looking for us, and they appeared to be disappointed.

I knew we must keep out of sight while waiting for a train out of Houston, so we boarded a street car, going as far south as we could go, where we waited till train time. This is where the train schedules I received the day before came in very handy. I already knew we could depart over the Houston & Texas Central train at eleven-five for Waco. I did not have to ask questions or go to the depot in advance.

Before boarding the train, we leisurely walked back and forth, concealing ourselves in the darkness, on the opposite side. We did not get on till the gong sounded. Then we boarded from the dark side of the train, where a door was open. The porter tried to stop us from entering but when I flashed a ten-dollar bill, he let us pass.

"You boarded from the wrong side," said the porter, as the train pulled out.

"I didn't have time to go around your dog-gonned train," I replied.

A murder had been committed at Hempstead a few minutes before our train arrived. The officers had information that the slayer was trying to escape

on our train, so that they were watching all passengers closely as we arrived. They searched the
train thoroughly.

I thought, of course, when I saw them board the
train with their guns in their hands, that they were
looking for us.

I had my arms folded, with my right hand on my
six-shooter, ready to fight; but I don't know whether
I was mad or scared. When I found out the officers
were looking for a murderer and not for me, I
joined in the search. I climbed on top and all over
the coaches, looking for the suspect.

We arrived at Waco the following morning about
eight o'clock. It was necessary to change cars there.
Officers were looking for us as we walked away from
the depot. Also a cousin of mine who lived at Waco
had been summoned to aid the officers. He could
identify me, but when I saw him at a distance I
stepped behind a signboard. We were standing on
a suspension bridge and, as the officers passed, they
eyed Pearlie closely. I felt sure they must have
known her but they said nothing and went ahead.
I didn't blame them at all for looking at the girl,
for I could hardly keep my eyes off her—she looked
like the prettiest girl in the world to me, and I was
willing to take almost any chance on earth to win
her. We managed to get aboard the train without
being caught and we arrived at Aquila, a station ten
miles from my father's home. There, in company
with my father, we hired a buggy, driving forty-five
miles to Cleburne. Father rode beside Pearlie and
I rode a horse.

I spent the happiest hours of my life in making
this drive to Cleburne. When we got to Cleburne,

we went to the Hamilton Hotel, where the marriage ceremony was performed by a justice of the peace. (This was on March 10, 1894.) In company with the justice, I stepped downstairs into the lobby of the hotel. There a deputy sheriff arrested me.

"Is your name Abernathy?" asked the deputy.

"You didn't skip it," I replied.

The deputy handed a telegram to me, addressed to the sheriff at Cleburne, which read: "Take charge and hold Jack Abernathy till further orders." The telegram was signed by the sheriff of Galveston.

"Well, Tom," said the justice of the peace, "you are too late; I just performed the marriage ceremony."

About this time my father came downstairs from the hotel parlor.

"Well, Pa, they got me," I said to him.

"Who's got you?" asked my father.

"The law has me."

"Mr. Abernathy," said the deputy, as his manner began to soften, "I want to ask you to go over and talk to the sheriff."

This was the only time in my life I ever stuttered. I said, "Well, let *me* go and tell," and as I stuttered some more, I continued, "tell my wife where I am going."

I walked with the deputy to the sheriff's office, and the deputy, upon entering the room, said, "Here is Jack Abernathy."

"Oh yes," said the Sheriff. "Have you that telegram?"

The deputy replied, "He has read it."

"Jack, what have you been doing?" asked the sheriff.

"I've been stealing the prettiest and smartest girl in Texas; yes, in the world!" I replied.

"Is that all you have stolen?"

"Isn't that enough?" I replied.

"Yes," said the sheriff, "I would like to see her."

I told the sheriff that I would be glad to take him over to the hotel to meet Mrs. Abernathy, the bride.

"She is mine by law," I said.

The sheriff, after meeting the bride, told me to take her home.

"If I want you, I will send for you," was his concluding remark.

Following our marriage, we made our home in Hill County for about eight months. Then we moved to Dallas, where I was engaged in business for six months. We next moved to Fort Worth, and made our home there for a year. I was employed as a piano and organ salesman, while my wife taught music. With our combined earnings we then bought a small herd of cattle and moved to old Greer County, Oklahoma. This was in 1898.

Some months before my settlement in Greer County I lost my mother. She was a wonderful woman, possessed of a keen mentality, which had been developed by a liberal education. Her spirituality and her faith in God were such that she knew no mental fears, though I was always the object of much anxiety on her part. Indeed, she had occasionally been heard to remark that she was quite sure that I would not die with my boots off.

CHAPTER IX

THE HUNT FOR A WHISKEY STILL

This adventure I fell into partly by accident. To be sure, when I met the Indian with the whiskey I could have let him go. But I was a deputy marshal, and I felt it my duty to enforce the law. The fact that the trail to the still took me out of my territory of Oklahoma into Arkansas didn't bother me: I remembered that as a citizen I had full authority to make the arrests.

The affair took place in the fall of 1899, when two Revenue officers came to Fort Smith, Arkansas, in search of a large still which was being operated about twelve miles west of the town. They hung around for a couple of days and got the general location and then decided to go out into the woods and "look around."

When they had almost reached the still, they discovered a boy about sixteen years old, red-headed and freckle-faced, sitting on a log, "picking" with his knife at it.

One of the men said,

"Hello, son, what are you doing down here? Watching the birds and the squirrels?"

The boy replied, "Nope! I'm watching my Daddy's still up the hollow there."

"Still! What is that?" asked one of the officers.

"Oh," he said, "it's where he makes moonshine whiskey."

"Oh yes, I've heard of those things," said the other

officer. "Son, I'll give you a dollar to show us the still. We never did see one."

"All right," said the boy, "give me the dollar."

The men started to go, saying, "Come on, let's go and see it." But the boy replied,

"Well, you haven't given me the dollar!"

"Oh," they said, "come on, won't you trust us? We'll give you the dollar when we come back."

The boy kept picking at the log, unconcernedly, and said to the officers,

"You'll give me the dollar now, for you're not coming back."

That declaration caused the officers to hesitate and look at each other. Stepping off to one side, one said,

"That kid was very positive in saying we weren't coming back; maybe we better go back to Fort Smith and get help and go at this thing right."

So they turned and said to the boy,

"Son, we'll give you the dollar when we come back next time. We'll see you again."

About an hour before this happened, as I learned later, I was riding from Oklahoma to Fort Smith. Just as I came to where I was to ford the Arkansas River, I met a Cherokee Indian with two sacks of whiskey tied on behind the saddle. I jerked my gun, "threw down on him," and said,

"Indian, you are under arrest! Put your hands up." He obeyed orders. "Now slide off that horse, and keep both hands up to the horn of the saddle." I then walked up and relieved him of the "45" that was in his belt. Upon closer searching I also found a little double-barreled Derringer in his right-hand coat pocket.   (I couldn't help but smile when I found that weapon.)   Then I said,

"Untie that whiskey and let it drop to the ground." While he was doing that he had his back to me, so I drew all the shells out of his "45" and put them in my pocket.   When he turned around, I handed him his empty gun, but of course he did not know it was empty.

"Now put this in your belt and leave it there," I said, "for if you try to get it, you will be a dead Indian.   Get your horse and take me to where you got this whiskey."   He obeyed orders.

We forded the Arkansas River, and within a mile reached the still.   Of course the Indian took me in the path that customers traveled.   When we arrived the two men who were in charge and who knew the Indian very well and thought I was another customer, didn't make any attempt to get their guns.

I dismounted and covered the men with both of my six-shooters.   I saw them glance at their guns leaning up against a tree not over ten feet away.

"Don't look at those guns," I said.   "You can't use them.   Walk over there and sit down on that bench."

I glanced at the Indian and said,

"Indian, jerk your gun!   What did I bring you along for?"   He obeyed.   I kept glancing around for other men, for from the looks of things around there I knew it took quite a number to operate the still. But luck was with me that day, for the owner (a "killer") was visiting a neighbor three miles away. However, I learned afterward that the two men under arrest were just as bad as they ever get to be—but I had got the drop on them and I kept it on them.

About that time up walked the red-headed, freckle-faced boy, with his hand lying on the handle of a "45." He evidently didn't see me, but he recognized the Indian, who was a customer. Seeing him with his gun drawn, the boy said,

"What does this mean?" At the same time he spied me. I switched one of my guns in his direction, saying at the same time,

"Put 'em up, kid, and put 'em up quick!" I then told the Indian to go get the kid's gun and bring it to me.

I spoke with authority because I knew I had to, and I was looking every minute for the ball to open.

"Indian," I said, "take that boy and go down to that house and get a wagon and team and bring it here quick."

In less than three-quarters of an hour they were back with a good team and wagon. I gave orders for them to load up. I had them put the worm in the wagon, along with several gallons of whiskey and several gallons of mash. I then made my two prisoners get into the wagon, told the Cherokee Indian to take the lines, and had the red-headed boy get on the Indian's horse and ride with me. This turned out to be lucky for me, for as we drove out from the still we had to pass by the owner's house, from which a woman ran out carrying a double-barreled shotgun and held up the procession. I said,

"Woman, drop that gun or I'll kill your boy" (I guessed it was her son), "and I don't mean maybe."

She dropped the gun—but that was one time I felt

uncomfortable—for I thought she might shoot me in the back as we rode away.

We had traveled about three miles when I noticed two men walking ahead of us, who proved to be the two Revenue officers previously mentioned. Their curiosity was aroused when they noticed the strange procession. As I passed them, one asked, "Are you an officer?"

"I don't skip it," I replied.

"Have you got these men under arrest?"

"Yep."

About that time one of the prisoners slugged the Indian, knocking him loose from the lines, and the other prisoner grabbed the lines and started the horses at break-neck speed. I threw spurs to my horse and shot ahead of them, firing a few shots from my gun, and stopped them.

This awakened the two Revenue officers, and they came as hard as they could toward us. I looked for my boy; he was riding for the timber at break-neck speed. I knew I couldn't catch him and keep the still and my two prisoners. The Revenue men ran up and I demanded,

"If you are officers, take charge of those prisoners, and one of you drive to Fort Smith just as quick as you can," for I realized the boy would notify the hill-billies and his Daddy, and I would have them to contend with.

Sure enough, in less than an hour, there were several men on horseback at the jail, with rifles and shotguns, inquiring for "the boy on the red roan horse." Of course I was that boy.

Seven years later, after I had become United

States Marshal of Oklahoma, and just after I had delivered a bunch of prisoners at Leavenworth, Kansas, and was walking through the Penitentiary in company with the Warden, a young man asked for permission to speak to me. This was granted. When I walked up to the young fellow, he asked,

"Don't you remember me?"

"No, son, I don't."

"I'm the boy who got away from you at Fort Smith, Arkansas."

"Are you doing time for that job?"

"No, I only got a year and a day, but Joe and Bob got fifteen years to do."

"What became of your Daddy?"

"They killed him about two years and a half after you grabbed that still, but he got three of them while they were killing him."

"Well, son, don't you see that crime doesn't pay?"

"Yes, I do, and if I ever get out of here, I'm going to live a different life."

CHAPTER X

HOMESTEADING IN OKLAHOMA

Two million acres, including some of the richest farm land in America located in the beautiful creek valleys surrounding the Wichita Mountains, were to be given away! This vast area was the famous Kiowa-Comanche-Apache and Wichita-Caddo Indian reservations. This land drawing was known as "President McKinley's Great Land Lottery." Millions of homeless people living in all parts of the nation read with great interest news of the huge drawing. All eyes were on Oklahoma, the last frontier.

To take part in this bit of our country's history was an experience never to be forgotten. I was doubly fortunate, for I saw the whole thing both as a homesteader and as a peace officer.

For a time it seemed as if the eagerly awaited drawing was not to be held at all. Chief Lone Wolf of the Kiowas sought to prevent the opening of the country by an injunction proceeding filed in the Oklahoma Federal Court. His appeal, however, was denied.

Unlike other land openings in Oklahoma, this one was not to consist of a "run" for homes, in which applicants literally raced one another from the border of the territory to the best sites. Earlier openings had resulted in many tragedies. Some of the racers had been killed, while others during the excitement had been shot down in bitter disputes over claims or following legal contests. The first murder committed after passage of the Oklahoma Capital Punishment Law was over a homestead contest. The murder took place on the steps of the land office in Guthrie, and the slayer was a legislator—a lower house member—who had been the author of the Capital Punishment Act.

The New Country, as the Kiowa-Comanche-Apache area was temporarily known, was opened under a Congressional Land Act* permitting citizens over the age of twenty-one to register and draw for the privilege of filing in turn. A great box mounted on shafting like an axle was used in the drawing, the lucky ones having the right to file in order as the names were drawn. The names, in envelopes, were shuffled until they were well mixed; then boys who were blind-folded drew out the envelopes one by one. Each envelope was then opened in the presence of the crowd, the name being read and then recorded by the clerks. A temporary enclosure was placed in front of the Irving school house in El Reno, where the largest number of persons registered. This enclosure was erected to avoid the danger of rain doing damage to records and papers. Another registration was conducted at Fort Sill. Five hundred names were drawn from each of the land offices the first day.

Under the law, homesteaders were required to live on the land drawn for five years from the date of filing, before they were entitled to a free deed from the Government. They were to till the soil, dig

---

*Dennis T. Flynn, delegate to Congress from Oklahoma Territory, introduced and secured passage of the bill providing for the great land lottery. He was among the great throng who failed to get a claim, his number being above sixty thousand, far in excess of the total number of farms distributed.

a well, and build a "habitable house." Six months
were allowed in order to make settlement, after
filing was recorded.   Homesteaders who desired to
commute and not to live on the land five years, could
pay a dollar and a quarter an acre within fourteen
months and receive a deed from the Government.
Soldiers of the Civil and Spanish-American wars
were allowed time off if they filed Old Soldiers'
Declarations.

Before the opening day for the "registration,"
in July, 1901, sixty thousand land seekers and fortune hunters swarmed into El Reno.   From ten to
twenty thousand had been camped for weeks, waiting for the registration to start.   This huge crowd
almost swamped the city, which ordinarily had a
population of about six thousand.   The summer of
1901 was hot and dry.   This was lucky for the home
seekers and "boomers," thousands of whom were
forced to sleep on vacant ground and on lawns and
porches of private houses.   Some residents of the
town rented space at fifteen cents each to persons
who slept on their porches.   This space did not in-
clude bedding of any kind.   Water sold at five cents
a tin cup during the heat of the day.   Nash Setzer,
a telegraph messenger boy at El Reno, earned eleven
dollars in one day carrying messages.

Railroads in Oklahoma were swamped in handling the crowds during the registration and New
Country boom.   The railroads hauled over four
hundred thousand people during three months.   Of
this great swarm, the roads serving El Reno handled
three hundred and twenty thousand inside of three
weeks.   Passengers rode on engines, tenders, tops of
cars, and on platforms of coaches.

The confusion was beyond description. During one trip from Oklahoma City to El Reno, a man impersonating the conductor on the old Choctaw train, went through several coaches, collected cash fares from the passengers, and kept the money. The depots were so crowded that it was almost impossible for a homesteader to buy a ticket. At the end of the registration, a total of over one hundred and sixty-seven thousand persons had signed up.

On August 6, 1901, the cities of Lawton, Anadarko, and Hobart were opened and the auction of lots began. I was at Lawton, having been sworn in as under-sheriff under Sheriff W. W. Painter. Lawton had the biggest assemblage of people before the lots were sold. The crowd camped outside the towns was estimated at more than twenty thousand.

I had my first real experience as a peace officer on the night of the opening. Two murders were committed and two men held for insanity. I arrested one of the murderers in front of the wagon yard the first night. This killing, like many other murders, was over a trivial matter. The prisoners were chained to a wagon and guarded, there being no jail of any kind.

Leslie P. Ross was elected mayor of Lawton; Heck Thomas, chief of police, and Hawkins, assistant chief. Thomas was an old-time hunter and frontier officer. In an earlier day he had been a deputy marshal in Oklahoma, also an express messenger on a train in Texas, when Sam Bass and his gang of outlaws staged a robbery. Assistant Chief Hawkins was six feet, six inches in height.

I found that being under-sheriff was a real man's job. Besides the lawless element with which I had to deal, there were the penniless, sick, and distressed persons to be looked after.   (There were, of course, no organized health department nor charitable institutions then.)   Lawton had fairly good water from wells, also from Medicine Creek.   The military post also had good water.   Despite this, however, there was a typhoid epidemic as in the other new towns, Hobart and Anadarko suffering the worst.

Lawton, where the land office was located, drew the biggest crowd of "boomers" after the registration closed.   The town had no railway until late in the following autumn, when the line from Anadarko was completed.   Thousands of dollars a day changed hands at Lawton in the sale of relinquishment rights on land claims.   A large percentage of the claim sellers went to saloons and gambling houses after being paid off.   Some managed to get away with part of their savings, but many lost all the cash they had received.

Not all the land was filed upon by homesteaders immediately.   I had not drawn a good number, but I filed on one of the overlooked tracts.   In settling on such a 160-acre tract, located in the north-east quarter of Section 29-1s-19w, which was in Comanche (now Tillman) County, I had plenty of opposition in establishing my right to the claim.   Six others sought to claim title to the same land.

The race started about eleven-thirty o'clock one night, from the west bank of the north fork of Red River.   The riders forded the river, and then raced east to the claim about two miles away.

I was driving a span of big horses hitched to a wagon containing a camping outfit, a large piano box, bedding, and cooking utensils.   My wife looked after the children, all of whom were small. She rode beside me, holding two of them in her arms as the team raced for the land.

The moment we arrived I unloaded the wagon and started digging a well. The piano box we set up as a "house" on the claim. It was large enough to hold my wife and children.

About one hundred yards to the east of our temporary home another land seeker started digging a well. His family did not arrive till the following day. This man, "Doc" Barr, mounted his horse in the night and rode to the Lawton Land Office, sixty-five miles away. He got there at nine o'clock the next morning, and filed on the land, claiming it as a homestead.

The three other contestants who had squatted on the land that night, kept up gun fire at frequent intervals while it was dark, attempting to frighten us. I was uneasy because of my wife and children. I told my wife that I would certainly open fire on them if they fired on us. I had a small arsenal close by while working in the well all night. I dug the hole, hitting the top of the water sand at twelve feet, before quitting that early morning.

Four of the contestants who did the firing during that night met me on the road as I was returning from Frederick—about two miles from the claim. This was three days after we had moved on the claim. This group stopped me, riding in front of my covered wagon. I was expecting trouble from these men, for I knew that two of them were notorious killers. They got off their horses and walked to within six feet of me.

"Well, Abernathy, some one has got to move," said one of them.

"You are not tied, are you?" I asked.

"Well, you can get into anything before you know it."

"And I can get out of it before you know it, too," I replied.

Another of the killers then chimed in:

"I have been tried three times for murder, and it isn't what it's cracked up to be."

I stepped out of the wagon, right in front of them, and said:

"Well, boys, I am going to tell you something, but you probably won't believe it. I never killed a man in my life!"

All this time, Blue Johnson, an old-time frontiersman, had been concealed inside my covered wagon. He had two double-barreled shotguns loaded with buckshot. Blue was a sharpshooter and was well known by this crowd of four as a real fighting man.

"Wow! Wow! Jack! Let's kill 'em all now!" shouted Blue, as he leaped from the back of the wagon to the front and took the drop on the quartet with one of the loaded shotguns. The other shotgun was within my easy reach.

"My God!" cried the leader of the quartet, as he looked down the barrel of Blue's shotgun, "you don't mean to murder us, do you?"

Blue Johnson then proceeded to tell the four men what he thought of them, in regular old-time cowboy language. I asked Blue not to shoot, and then said:

"Now boys, I moved on that claim to stay. When I move off, I'll be hauled off; so if there is any moving

going to take place, I would advise you to move—
and move fast."

Six weeks later after this race for the land, our
fifth baby was born, in the dugout on the homestead.
This baby, a girl, was named Jack by her mother.

Later, in the trial before the Land Office officials
at Lawton, I was awarded title to the land, after they
heard the story about the piano-box house, and the
birth of the baby. These two incidents, the Land
Office officials said, established beyond doubt all
question of actual settlement.

I immediately started building a house for my
family, hauling the lumber from Vernon, Texas,
a distance of fifty-eight miles. It was necessary to
ford three rivers in hauling the lumber—the North
Fork of Red, the Red, and the Peace River. The
lumber was hauled when the streams were low.
After the house was finished, I bought two cows,
eighteen hens and a rooster—the beginning of life
on the new homestead.

One of the cows was a strawberry roan and the
meanest animal to kick I ever heard tell of. She
gave four gallons of milk a day when fresh; but I
had to rope her by the head to a post, then tie both
hind legs to another post, and pull her down. After
I had milked two teats, I had to turn her over and
repeat the performance, in order to get the rest of
the milk. But we had to have it.

I had bad luck with the chickens because of the
wolves, which began robbing the roosts. One by
one the hens disappeared, till all were gone. Only
a Dominique rooster was left of the flock.

Early one morning, after returning home from

playing for a dance, I was dozing across the foot of the bed.   Mrs. Abernathy was getting breakfast when she screamed out that she saw a wolf.

"There goes our rooster," she cried.

Half asleep, I rolled out of bed, grabbed my six-shooter, and ran to the yard.   There I saw the wolf carrying the rooster in its mouth, perhaps seventy-five paces from the house.   Holding the gun in both hands, I fired.   I managed to wound the wolf, so that he dropped the rooster.   The latter, with both wings dragging the ground, made a bee line toward me. He had never been a pet, but for the moment he recognized me as a friend.

CHAPTER XI

I BRING BACK A KILLER

Before long I had to deal with worse than wolves. The Bert Casey gang had robbed the post office at Marlow, Indian Territory, in August, and one of the bandits had been killed by a posse. Shortly afterwards the same gang held up a stage coach which made regular trips from Rush Springs, Indian Territory, to the New Country. The robbery was staged about half-way between Rush Springs and Lawton. While searching the passengers on the stage, one of the bandits shot and killed the young son of Dr. Z. E. Beemblossom, of Oklahoma City.

As a member of the sheriff's force I joined in the search for Bert Casey and his outlaw gang, which terrorized the Twin Territories from 1901 until 1904. I was associated with Sheriff Frank Smith and Deputy George Beck, of Anadarko, both of whom were murdered the day after Christmas, 1901, near Fort Cobb, Caddo County. The sheriff and deputy were killed trying to arrest the outlaws, who had taken refuge in an abandoned ranch house.

I was now appointed a deputy under U. S. Marshal Bill Fossett, my work being confined to the field in Comanche and other south-western counties.

I was notified one day by telegram from headquarters at Guthrie, to meet Deputy Marshal Fry, in Lawton. He said to me:

"We have a bad man to arrest, who is hiding in a dugout in the Wichita Mountains. We must go to

90

the Supervisor of the Forest Reserve, to find out just where the dugout is located."

The Forest Supervisor was thirty-five miles away. We hired a livery rig, pulled by two wild and snaky horses, and drove to the headquarters of the Reserve.

"I'll bet you boys are after Keller," said the Supervisor.

"Yes."

"I'm sorry for you. Keller never will be taken alive."

I learned from the Supervisor where the dugout was. In order to get to the place we had to go back fifteen miles to Cache. Then we had to go west eight miles, to Indiahoma; then north fifteen miles to the dugout.

Just as we drove into Cache, the passenger train bound for Lawton came in from the west. As it pulled into the depot, Deputy Fry took the warrant out of his pocket and said to me:

"You get him if you can. I've got to go to Lawton."

I then took the warrant, and drove to the farm of Jim Simmons, district farmer for the Comanche Indians. I spent the night with Simmons, telling him of my job, and inviting him to go along.

"My father went with a deputy one time, to arrest a bad man in Missouri, and had to kill the man," said Simmons, "and he came near never getting out of the trouble."

I told Simmons that he need not go along. However, I asked him to help me by serving certain subpoenas on Indians; also to have the horses ready at five o'clock in the morning to go after Keller. Simmons at first said he would not let me go after Keller alone. But he had the horses ready to go early on the following morning.

After driving eight miles west and ten miles north, just as I left the homestead area, I saw a man dodge behind a house. I called him over and asked him about the location of a certain claim.

"I know you very well," he said. "You are John Abernathy, Deputy U. S. Marshal. I know you are after Keller. You also kept the conductor on the train from Snyder to Lawton from kicking my ribs out the other night."

I said to him, "You are just the man I want to go along with me." I persuaded him to get into the buggy and go along to where we could locate the dugout. We traveled about eight miles. The country near the dugout was very rough, being covered with heavy timber and underbrush. He pointed out a spot about a mile distant near a mountain peak, as the spot. He then left me.

I drove ahead about one hundred and fifty yards; then stopped, and tied the tongue of the buggy to a tree. (This was the only safe way to tie wild horses.) It was just a little after sun-up that morning when I tied the team.

Taking my rifle out of the buggy, I started at a pretty fast walk, for I was anxious to get the job done. I came to a mountain stream with running water and I waded this cold water, waist deep. I kept my eyes on the peak, but failed to find the dugout or any signs of civilization. Dropping back one hundred and fifty yards to the south-west, I made my way back to the horses. Although greatly disappointed at the time, I afterward regarded my failure to locate the dugout that hour in the morning as very fortunate, for this outlaw would have had every advantage of me in the dugout.

I rested for a while, then thought to myself, "I've got to get my man." I waded the creek again, but this time I went a little farther to the north-west, as I began searching the underbrush. I was clipping along quietly over a path which led through the brush when I heard the sound of some one chopping wood. I knew this must be Keller: there was nobody else living within ten miles of the place. I could hear about five licks on the log with the axe, then a delay of a moment or two. I took this to mean that the wood chopper was scouting between licks to see if any one was near.

I kept slipping along through the underbrush, until finally I saw a little open place. From the sound of the axe I could tell that the chopper was right on the edge of the brush, just a short distance away. I knelt down on my knees to examine my six-shooter. As I did so, I said, to myself, "God have mercy upon us," and got up. I advanced about ten steps, then stepped out into the open. There stood Keller!

I took a dead bead on him, shouting at the top of my voice,

"Hands up, Keller!"

He did not move. He just stood there, looking at me like a mean bull. There was no time to lose: I pulled the trigger of my rifle. This was all I could do, since he disobeyed my command. But my rifle only snapped! Never before had I had a gun snap when I pulled the trigger.

Like lightning, I had pumped another cartridge into the barrel, cursing Keller as I did so. Then

Keller started slowly to put up his hands. I forced him to back away from the axe, and kept myself between him and his gun. He had his coat off and I was sure that he was without a weapon of any kind.

I discovered that Keller's six-shooter was on the ground under his vest, which he had removed while chopping, so I walked sideways, holding my rifle on him, until I could pick up the pistol.

"I have thirteen guns trained on you, Keller," I said. "If you make a wrong move, you will drop dead in your tracks! Now, turn your face to the west and step lively. If you make an awkward move, I'll call my men out of the brush."

I could have dropped Keller, but I did not want to, so I ran my bluff and made it stick. I forced him to hit the path and keep looking ahead. As he walked in front of me, I let him put down his hands.

After a half-mile of marching, Keller started to talk but I told him each time to shut up. When we arrived at the mountain stream, Keller asked me what to do. I said,

"Hit the water and hit it hard."

Keller waded the water with his clothes on and I followed. This was my fourth time that day I had waded this cold stream.

I knew better than to try to handcuff Keller while marching him down from the hideout. Had I tried to do this without help, he would have got me. He was a brawny Kentucky mountaineer fighter, weighing about one hundred and ninety pounds, and without a pound of extra fat. From every appearance he was more than my equal in physical strength. He was seven inches taller than I, being six feet, two inches in height.

Keller kept looking for the men of whom I had told him. I forced him to untie the team, then made him come back on the same side of the buggy I was on. He got inside and I sat down, jammed up against him. I did the driving with my left hand, holding my right hand on my pistol. I also had Keller's pistol and my rifle beside me. Keller tried to look back but I told him to look ahead. As we drove to the homestead area, Keller said to me,

"If you hadn't told me that . . . . lie, I wouldn't be here."

"Yes, you would: you would be here—but in a different shape."

I drove to Cache with Keller as my prisoner, where Simmons, the Comanche district farmer, was waiting with one hundred armed Indians.

He told me it had been his plan to start the Indians on a search of the underbrush and mountains.

I gave Simmons a wink. He caught it, and came around to my side of the buggy. I whispered to him, "Put the cuffs on Keller." He did, and I took a long breath of relief.

In company with the Indians, for whom attachments had been issued, I went on to Guthrie. Marshal Bill Fossett then sent me to Covington, Kentucky, with Keller, who had escaped jail there while under sentence of death for killing three persons. Three weeks later he was executed.

CHAPTER XII

ROOSEVELT BECOMES INTERESTED

Even while I was serving as deputy marshal, I occasionally got permission to put on a wolf hunt at some public meeting. One such event I took part in at Lyon's Park, between Sherman and Denison, Texas. My wolf catch was the big feature of the two-day event ending on Christmas Day, 1904.

The event stands out in my memory for two reasons. The first is that on that day I had one of my few mishaps in capturing my wolf.

I had become exceedingly tired by the final day of the entertainment. Between performances I ran into the box office at the park to get a drink of water. The ticket seller offered me a drink of whiskey, saying:

"Jack, you look tired! Have a little swig of this; it won't hurt you."

I swallowed a big drink and quickly returned to the grounds. Almost at once I had my dog Cannon Ball and the wolf released for the final catch. (The dog was so named because it would not tackle a wolf until after a gun had been fired.)

"Take the saddle off," shouted a dozen or more in the grandstand, as the race started. I jerked off the saddle, leaping onto my horse bare-back.

The dog raced the wolf around the track three times, remaining side by side with the "loafer" without offering to bite until it heard my shot. At the crack of my pistol, Cannon Ball grabbed for the wolf

THE END OF THE LAST RACE ON THE PRESIDENT'S HUNT

THE ABERNATHY KIDS

and the fight was on. A moment later I leaped for the "loafer," and the crowd cheered wildly. I thrust my right hand into his mouth as usual, and straddled him with my legs. I was looking back to see if the Negro helpers were coming with the wire to tie his jaws, when suddenly the wolf bit my hand. I hurled my pistol to the ground, and went after the "loafer" for keeps. Again grabbing the wolf, I "clinched" it, and held it firmly till the Negroes came up.

I believe it was the whiskey which caused me to have this accident. Right there I took an oath to never again take a drink when I had a wolf to catch or a bad man to capture. Whiskey or any other kind of liquor slows one's speed, dims his eye and makes him nervous.

The second reason why I remember that Christmas day is that it led indirectly to my friendship with Theodore Roosevelt. My wolf catches there at Lyons Park had attracted lots of attention, and had been watched with much interest by the owner of the Park, Col. Cecil A. Lyon. Now Colonel Lyon was both a National Guard Commander and a National Republican Committeeman, and through these conditions had come to know President Roosevelt well. They had become great hunting companions, and it was through this common interest that Colonel Lyon told Mr. Roosevelt about seeing a Texas cowboy catch wolves with his bare hands.

At first the President thought Colonel Lyon was joking. When he learned that this was not so, he expressed the wish to see the trick performed.

Plans were already under way for the President to hunt in Texas and Louisiana, with Colonel Lyon as host. The President now wrote a letter to me asking

me to stage a wolf hunt for him. Of course I readily
agreed. The time selected for the arrival of the
President and his party was April 5, 1905. The
entertainment was to last six days.

I had selected Big Pasture as the most desirable
place. The nearest train depot was Frederick. So
I mounted my favorite horse, Sam Bass, and with the
wolf dogs, six in number, was off for Frederick.

I had engaged George Nichols of Frederick to help
me to look after the dogs. Nichols was quite used
to wolf hunts, having gone with me many times.
We placed a cage on an Indian hack to haul the dogs
to the hunting ground. We made every effort to
conserve the strength of the dogs for the chase.

I arrived at Frederick about noon on April 5th,
very proud to think the President of the United States
had sought me out. I was to be the star performer
on a six-day hunt, perhaps the most novel event ever
staged in honor of a President. Despite the large
publicity, and the fuss made over me, I thought but
little more of what I was to do than I had thought of
doing on scores of other days. It was the honor of
staging a hunt for this great man that appealed
to me.

I had made all arrangements for the chase. I had
selected a camp site at a point located eighteen miles
east of Frederick, on Deep Red Creek. The grounds
were picturesque. The region abounded in game,
and Deep Red Creek was one of the best for fishing.

Soldiers from Fort Sill Military Reservation were
on duty, patrolling the border of the Big Pasture
Reserve. This was done to keep away the crowds of
curious spectators who might interfere with the President's sport. Newspaper men and photographers

were not included in the party, but two members of the President's party carried cameras. I want right here to express my thanks to Dr. Alexander Lambert, of New York City, former physician to Theodore Roosevelt, for the use in this book of several pictures which he took at that time.

Frederick looked forward with feverish interest to having the President spend a week in its vicinity. Great crowds gathered in the street waiting for the arrival of his train.

CHAPTER XIII

ENTERTAINING THE PRESIDENT

The President arrived about two o'clock in the afternoon. A grand stand had been erected and was packed with people waiting to catch a glimpse of him. American flags hung from every house and building in the little town. Several bands were playing and hundreds cheering as the President appeared on the platform of the train. He stopped, saluted the crowd, and waved his hat. Then he stepped into a waiting carriage and was driven to the grand stand two blocks away.

I had several wagons at the train and supervised unloading the baggage and hunting equipment for the camp. By the time I had mounted Sam Bass and ridden to the grand stand, the President was making a speech. Among those seated on the grand stand with the President were: Col. Cecil A. Lyon; Captain S. Burke Burnett and Tom Waggoner, noted Texas ranchman; Lieutenant B. L. Fortesque, U. S. A., formerly of the Rough Riders; Lieut. Gen. S. B. M. Young, U. S. A., retired; Dr. Alexander Lambert of New York, the President's physician; Sloan Simpson, former Rough Rider; and Quanah Parker, Chief of the Comanche Indians, with three of his wives and one baby.

I rode up toward the grand stand on Sam Bass, and the crowd gave way. I rolled out of the saddle, dropping the bridle reins on the ground. Climbing the steps, I made my way toward the President.

Colonel Lyon, seeing me, interrupted the President in his speech, exclaiming:

"Here comes the wolf catcher, Mr. President!"

President Roosevelt turned to me and said,

"You look like a man who could catch a wolf. I want to congratulate you, for I know you are going to do what Colonel Lyon says you can do."

He then gave me a hearty handshake. This was the beginning of a lasting friendship.

As he finished his speech, he said,

"I came down here for a quiet hunt and rest, and I do hope and trust that I will not be bothered while in the Big Pasture."

An hour later the party was off to the wolf grounds. Everything was in readiness for the party when the camp was reached that night. Pullman car waiters and cooks from the train furnished the meals at the camp. A long table was spread in the dining tent. There were about fifteen tents in the camp. A street was laid off, the President's tent being on one side adjoining one occupied by myself and C. B. McHugh, a banker from Frederick. In the President's tent, he and Dr. Lambert slept. Across the tent street from these two, the others in the party slept, two men to each tent.

After dinner a big wood fire was built between the two groups of tents in the street, and everybody gathered around the fire. The President led off with the story telling the first night. He told of his early days as a cowboy and ranchman in the wilds of North Dakota. He told how he went West in the early days in order to regain his health. It was during the time spent on the frontier of the old West, he said, that he had become so fond of outdoor sports, and had gained a lasting respect for western life.

I was amazed at the President's knowledge of wild animals, snakes, and even the smallest of reptiles and insects. In telling stories about reptiles, he described in detail the difference between the poisonous and non-poisonous. He told of the vinegaroon, the most deadly of the poisonous creatures in Texas and Old Mexico; many of those old-time hunters present had never even heard of such a reptile. He asked me if I had ever seen one, and I told him I guessed I had seen hundreds of them while I was on the range.

About ten-thirty the story telling ended and everybody went to bed. It was agreed that breakfast should be served at daylight, when the first chase was to be started.

The next morning horses were fed and saddled for us as soon as breakfast was over. We all mounted and rode south of the camp, where we sighted a coyote. There were about twelve riders in this race. We had not been racing more than ten minutes before this coyote jumped into Little Red—water about four feet deep. (A wolf or coyote can fight better in water than on dry land, and seems to have an advantage over dogs.)

I was glad the first event was staged in water, in order that the President might see how a wolf could conquer a dog. This coyote cut several of the dogs very badly and came near drowning one of them. The President rode within twenty feet and was watching every move made. I, too, was standing at the edge of the water watching the fight. About ten minutes after the fight started, the dogs killed this coyote.

I took the lead alongside the President as the riders started again traveling south toward Red River. Soon we sighted two gray wolves about half a mile ahead. Inside another mile and a half of chasing, I leaped from my horse, caught the wolf by the under jaw, and held the animal up so that the President could see him.

"Bully!" exclaimed the President. "I haven't been skunked. This catch pays me for the trip to Oklahoma and corroborates Colonel Lyon's statement. But, say, isn't that wolf biting you?"

"No. It *is* hurting a little, but the teeth are doing no real damage," was my reply. The President examined the wolf's lips and saw the position of my hand, with the canine teeth in front of it.

"Oh, I see now," he said. "But how do you get your hand behind those teeth?"

"By practice, Mr. President."

The jaws of this wolf were then wired, and the animal placed inside the cage on the dog hack. Then the party met the chuckwagon and lunch was served on the prairie. The air was cool and the day was ideal.

In the afternoon I made a second catch. Afterwards there was considerable discussion among the riders as to just how the catch could be made every time. The President said:

"I can't quite understand just all about this yet."

"Well, Mr. President," I responded, "you must remember that a wolf never misses its aim when it snaps. When I strike at a wolf with my right hand, I know it is going into the wolf's mouth. I believe I could shut my eyes and do what you see me do, for

I have caught two wolves in my life in inky darkness However, I prefer *not* to shut my eyes."

After supper that night the main discussion was about the manner in which the wolves had been caught. I heard a heated argument around the camp fire as I was looking after Sam Bass, my horse. A bet had been made, I afterwards learned, between Colonel Lyon and Al Bivens, a wealthy cattleman from Amarillo. It developed later that Bivens had been brought there to catch a wolf, hoping to outdo me. When I came up to the camp fire, Colonel Lyon said:

"Jack, will you let Al have the first race in the morning?"

"Yes, sir—and the second one too, if he wants it."

Both Bivens and Lyon held checks in their hands and were standing close together at the time.

"Bivens says he will catch a wolf like you do—just like you do, without getting bitten; and I have offered to give him this five-hundred-dollar check if he does," continued Lyon.

"Oh, Colonel, there wasn't anything said about being bitten," interrupted Bivens.

"Well, I thought there was. However, if you will catch the wolf and wire his mouth up, I don't care how much the wolf bites you—the five hundred is yours."

Lyon added that if Bivens didn't catch the wolf as I did, Bivens would give Lyon a check for five hundred dollars. President Roosevelt was standing within two feet of Lyon when this conversation took place. Lyon offered to let the President hold the stakes, but he refused.

On the next morning the riders got an early start,

all being in the saddle at sun-up. The President on this ride was alongside Bivens, in the lead of the riders. Bivens took nine dogs along with him—six greyhounds and three staghounds. I thought that the dogs would eat Bivens up—there were so many. However, I said nothing.

After we had gone a mile and a half we sighted three coyotes. The chase was on. Bivens started at break-neck speed, followed closely by the dogs. They singled out the smallest coyote of the three, which is something unusual.

I was not supposed to take the lead, and was trying to hold Sam Bass back. But Sam Bass wasn't in the habit of letting other horses take the lead; so I arrived on the scene of the fight about one hundred yards ahead of Bivens. I turned sidewise after stopping, watching the nine dogs try to kill the little coyote. The coyote was wet from slobber from the dogs when Bivens leaped from the horse. Bivens tried to thrust his left hand into the coyote's mouth, but the animal shut down on his thumb before he could do so. Bivens then grabbed the coyote with his right hand, pulling his thumb out and splitting the nail. Doctor Lambert leaped from his horse and attempted to throw his right hand into the coyote's mouth as he had seen me do, but he was too slow. The coyote buried its canine teeth into the fleshy part of the Doctor's hand. The Doctor jerked out his hunting knife with his left hand and stabbed the coyote to the heart.

The President was close beside Bivens, who was standing about six feet away, sucking his injured thumb. I slid out of my saddle and walked around to Bivens, saying:

"Let me tend your thumb. I wouldn't suck it. I know what a wolf bite is. He might have had a decayed tooth and this might poison you."

"You are the last man on earth I thought would want to do anything for me," replied Bivens.

"I don't care what you said about me, Bivens, I want to doctor your sore thumb," I said, as I produced a clean handkerchief and applied the wolf medicine, dressing the wound.

President Roosevelt, who listened to the conversation and saw me dress Biven's wound, remarked:

"Abernathy, I guess it is up to you from here on out."

Just then the dog wagon drove up and I said,

"Mr. President, come around here and pick out one dog. I will catch the next wolf."

"No! No!" replied the President. "I can see what power these coyotes have in their jaws; you must take three or four dogs, because here were nine dogs and two men were bitten."

"Mr. President," I protested, "please don't burden me with dogs. Really, I need only one dog, for all I want the dog to do is to stop the wolf and give me time to get off my horse."

However, I compromised with the President and he was satisfied. I agreed to take two dogs, neither of which had ever yet stopped a wolf. (These two were the fastest dogs I had.)

We started in a south-easterly direction, and I soon sighted a wolf going toward Red River. I knew if we kept riding we would make close contact. I had also sighted an eagle on the ground over to the west and asked the boys (without saying what the object was) to watch it closely, because it might be a wolf. I did this to keep them looking, for I didn't want them to see the wolf I wanted to catch. I wanted a short race, since neither of these dogs had ever caught a wolf. My scheme worked. We got within a hundred yards of the wolf before the boys noticed it. Just as they hallooed, I spoke to my two little dogs and they went off like bullets, speeding after the wolf. As the black greyhound passed in front of the wolf so fast that it could not turn, the wolf fleshed its canine teeth in the hound's shoulder and split a gash six inches in length. The President saw and heard the stroke, which sounded like tearing a piece of ducking.

When I leaped to the ground, the wolf sprang at me, and in an instant I had the animal at arm's length. This was one of the prettiest catches that I ever made.

The President ran up and said:

"Abernathy, this looks as if it were mechanically done."

Doctor Lambert was present with his kodak. The President asked all the boys to stand back, saying,

"I want this picture with just Abernathy and myself in it."

"Mr. President," said the Doctor, "you can say that this picture was snapped about a minute from the time Abernathy started the chase and made the catch."

CHAPTER XIV

MY WILDEST RIDE

Colonel Lyon, who was responsible for the wolf hunt staged in honor of the President, understood the feeling of rivalry that resulted from my success in catching wild, snapping wolves with my bare hands—a feat nobody else has ever been able to duplicate. The climax of this jealousy developed during the first two days of this hunt.

I was never worried for a moment as to my own success or the ability of my trained horse, Sam Bass, and the wolf dogs. The trained animals, which had a big part in the success of the chase, were the best to be found on the prairies. I was quite confident that I not only had the fastest running horse, but also that my dogs could not be beaten.

Captain S. Burke Burnett, Tom Waggoner, Al Bivens, and their dare-devil riders were all jealous from the start, for they saw that I was taking the lead in nearly every race that was staged. (Burnett and Waggoner were two of the oldest and richest of the pioneer Texas ranchmen and Bivens was also very wealthy.)

Burnett and Waggoner, both famous as owners of the very finest and most beautiful blooded horses that Texas could produce, brought the cream of their thoroughbreds for the wolf chase. Both placed their choicest racing animals at the disposal of the President. Every day he, as well as Burnett and Waggoner, had a fresh blooded racer for every event, while I was forced to rely entirely upon the training, strength, and racing ability of Sam Bass.

Tom Burnett, son of Burke, who was to take part in the events of the third day, was one of my most bitter and determined rivals. His attitude recalled a near fight he and I had had in a saloon at Wichita Falls. After the President first wrote me about staging the wolf hunt, Tom Burnett had wired me to meet him in Wichita Falls. I met Tom in the saloon and we talked it all over. Tom wanted me to have the chase on the Burke Ranch near Electra, Texas, but I refused. He offered me one thousand dollars. I told Tom, in refusing the offer, that this was a lot of money—a mighty sum to me, a poor boy from Oklahoma—but that, if we held the race on the Burnett Ranch, our lives would be endangered by the mesquite bushes which covered the ranch. I pointed out that we had open prairie in the Big Pasture, making it much safer for the race. I told Tom I did not want to have an accident, especially since the President had placed so much confidence in me.

Tom became very angry when I refused to accept the thousand and he began talking pretty rough. It made me angry, and finally, before the owners of the saloon put us both out, I said to him:

"I do not believe in selling the safety of the President for one thousand dollars or any other amount."

I left and went around a block for a walk to cool off. Coming back, I saw Tom on the other side of the street. I felt that there might be more trouble, but I went on to meet him. When we met, Tom extended his hand, offering to shake and be friends.

"I guess it would be pretty dangerous," he said,

referring again to the proposed chase. "Perhaps we should hold the race in Oklahoma. I have wired Colonel Lyon to meet me here tonight. He will arrive on the midnight train and we will have it out." I had no trouble in convincing Colonel Lyon that the proper place for the race was in the Big Pasture.

On the evening after the second day's chase, Colonel Lyon called me over to one side of the camp, suggesting that a test race be held to settle the feeling of rivalry.

"The boys have it in for you, as big as a mule," said the Colonel, "and they have not tried to conceal their bitterness even from the President. We have decided to have a test race, to find out who is the most skilful, and who has the fastest horse and dogs. We will take two dogs from each pack and the riders will be cut down to a total of seven. The President and I will not be included. This race will be too fast for me."

"Very well, Colonel, I am more than willing to agree to such a test race," was my reply. "I want you to understand, however, that I have not said anything about what I could do. I hope the boys don't carry this too far."

On the morning of the third day, the riders had breakfast before daylight and were in the saddle at sun-up. We started south-west from the camp toward Red River. As we had left the camp, the President and I had taken the lead, riding beside each other. We were followed by the others who were about one hundred yards behind. (This was the general line-up during the entire six days.)

Soon I sighted a wolf, and a moment later the others saw it, too.

"Yonder is a wolf; I wonder why Abernathy don't catch it," said Tom Waggoner. He was evidently trying to make fun of me. This made me very angry, but I held in. In a few minutes I heard Waggoner repeat the remark, adding,

"I thought Abernathy was going to catch everything that jumped up."

At this, I reined in my horse and stopped, the President also halting beside me. The other riders came up. Turning in my saddle, I faced Waggoner and said:

"Mr. Waggoner, I never said what I could do. We don't get the President of the United States to come to Oklahoma every year; this race is to be a test race. But I am here to tell you now, that I *can* catch everything that jumps up, if you force me to say it, and right here is a good place to start it."

I leaped from my horse and grabbed Waggoner's horse by the reins, proceeding to tell the multi-millionaire cattleman "how the cow ate the cabbage, stalk and all."

President Roosevelt was sitting within six feet of both of us, and when he saw that Waggoner was not going to dismount, he spoke up very spiritedly,

"Abernathy, get on your horse!"

"All right, Mr. President. If the court so rules, I bow."

Again the riders took their positions and started on.

President Roosevelt broke the silence by saying:

"I want you to understand, Mr. Abernathy, that I came to Oklahoma to run wolves with you. Don't let anyone start you till you get ready. By George, I don't believe they will!"

I was so utterly disgusted that I was afraid to talk, so I said no more till the President said:

"Do you believe that you can catch that particular wolf?"

"Yes, Mr. President; but it is going to be a long race."

As wolves sometimes do, this one was walking around watching the riders. The President said:

"I do not know what I would give to see you catch that wolf."

"All right, Mr. President, you flag 'em ahead," I said.

President Roosevelt took off his hat and waved it, shouting, "Go get him," and the riders were off in a wild race.

Tom Burnett, Bony Moore, Al Bivens, Fi Taylor, Doctor Lambert, Tom Waggoner, and Lieutenant Fortescue all shot at full speed past the President and me, leaving us well in the rear.

The President was a bit in the lead as the other riders passed us. I was pulling Sam's head against his breast. He was making an effort to take the lead as usual. I was riding with my weight on the back of his neck, protecting him all I could. By bearing my weight partly on my hands, I took most of the load off the saddle, thus saving his wind and strength. I had learned that this increased his endurance by about one-fourth, especially in a long race. And from the manner in which that wolf started, I knew we were in for a long run.

The President was mounted on a dove-colored horse from the Waggoner ranch. It was perhaps the

QUANAH PARKER, CHIEF OF THE COMANCHES, AND THREE OF
HIS WIVES. HE TAUGHT THE AUTHOR HOW TO TRAIL
HORSE THIEVES

THE AUTHOR SHOWING TEDDY ROOSEVELT HOW TO HOLD A
LIVE WOLF

THE ABERNATHY KIDS (FIVE AND NINE) ENROUTE ALONE TO
NEW YORK CITY TO GREET TEDDY ROOSEVELT

mightiest racing steed of the entire string of blooded racers owned by Waggoner.

When the wolf saw the riders start, it began running, and how they can run! The pace continued for about two and a half miles. I began to notice that some of the dare-devil riders, who had taken the lead at first, were beginning to show signs of slackening their speed. All were whipping their horses on the hairy side (the left, which is seldom touched with a whip). When we had gone about three miles, the horses ahead began wringing their tails. (This was indication that they had about "shot their bolts.")

I had managed to hold Sam Bass back by talking to him, and by patting him once in awhile. Sam seemed to understand it all—that I was about to let him loose to do his stuff. I knew Sam Bass and he knew me.

The President, Doctor Lambert, and I were about two hundred yards behind the others. I turned to my two companions and said: "Let's let them stop," meaning by this that we would take the lead.

Sam Bass soon shot ahead of the others, leaving the President next nearest, closely followed by Doctor Lambert. To my surprise, I could see that the wolf was still half a mile ahead. We rode another mile, then came to a draw where the banks were from two to three feet high. I knew that a wolf when crowded always takes to rough ground. This one started right up the draw, which made it more difficult for the horses to follow at full speed.

We jumped our horses over the bluff. By this time the three of us were about two miles ahead of the rest of the party. Only one dog was left in the chase—my own blue bitch.

I looked back at the President as I jumped Sam Bass over the rough ground. Roosevelt was a superb rider and could certainly handle the dove-colored racer. I realized that I was making a dangerous ride; but, though my life was in danger, the President of the United States was taking every chance that I was taking.

The wolf turned out over a prairie-dog town, then crossed over to another draw. In going through this dogtown, Sam Bass would make both long and short jumps, dodging the holes. Had Sam stepped into one of the holes, we would have gone down and no doubt lost the race, but he continued to jump, sometimes leaping fully fifteen feet.

In pursuing the wolf as it made another turn, I lost sight of the President. I was within forty steps of the wolf, watching it closely. I thought I would run ahead of the wolf hoping that I could make the catch with my hands without the aid of the dog.

The wolf leaped up at me as I crossed ahead of it and caught me by the foot, splitting my boot. Then it fell. I heard somebody yell. Looking back over my shoulder, I saw the President about one hundred yards off. He was riding more gracefully than the most experienced race rider at a Derby, whipping his horse on the hairy side.

At this instant, my little blue bitch, getting back into the race, nipped the wolf, and the wolf slashed her. At the next turn made, I leaped off the back of Sam Bass, catching the wolf in the usual way.

There wasn't a dog within twenty feet when I

leaped out of the saddle. When I got my usual hold, the President leaped from his racer and ran to me.

"I would like to shake hands with you!" shouted the President when he came near where I was holding the wolf. "I do wish you could get that right hand free."

I shoved my left thumb into the wolf's mouth, prying the jaws apart. Then I grabbed the jaw with my left hand, freeing my right. I then reached up with my right, shaking hands with the President.

"Has the wolf hurt you?"

"No," I replied.

"This beats anything I have ever seen in my life, and I have seen a good deal!" exclaimed the President.

Looking back, we observed Doctor Lambert, Bony Moore, and Tom Burnett. They were about two miles away, but were coming as fast as their jaded horses could carry them.

Waving his hat and yelling at the top of his voice, the President saluted the riders as they came up.

"Now, Doctor, what did I tell you last night?" asked the President.

"What did I tell you, Mr. President?" laughed Dr. Lambert.

I did not know what the President and Doctor had been talking about the night before. I was sitting astride the wolf, having retaken a hold of the animal's jaw with my right hand.

"Abernathy, Sam Bass, and the blue bitch!" exclaimed the President.

"And the President of the United States!" added Dr. Lambert.

I had lost the wire used for holding the wolf's

jaws; so I continued to hold him with my right hand, catching his hind legs with my left. It was embarrassing. Throwing the wolf over Sam's back, I mounted and Doctor Lambert picked up the reins, and placed them in my teeth. Thus we started for the surreys where most of the party had gathered, two miles away. Sam Bass started to gallop, and I had difficulty bringing him to a stop: he thought another wild race was on. He shot past the surreys, and I had to manage to get my left hand free long enough to pull him around in a circle. Both my hands were pretty much occupied holding the wolf. However, I managed to stop by the time the President had dismounted.

"Tom, you should congratulate Abernathy," said the President, addressing Waggoner.

"Well, I will," replied Waggoner, "but I want first to see what that horse is made out of. Steel and the best of steel."

That night the President drank my health in grape juice at the camp fire.

This day's ten-mile race forever settled the dispute between the big ranchmen and myself. At the camp fire that night the President examined my boot, observing the two-inch gash that the wolf had cut. He again spoke of the quickness of hand which was necessary to catch the wolf without getting bitten.

CHAPTER XV

THE FINISH OF THE PRESIDENT'S HUNT

On the fourth morning of the hunt, I said to Mr. Roosevelt,

"Mr. President, I just saw one of the biggest wolves I've ever seen go right under the hill over there into the big wild onion flat."

"Bully," shouted the President, "let's go get it!"

The riders quickly assembled and we were off. We were within one hundred and fifty yards of the wolf before it broke and ran back west toward Little Red Creek. Had the ground been smooth, we could have made the catch before we had gone a mile, but it was full of cracks which were very dangerous for the horses, and we could not race at full speed. One horse fell, throwing his rider.

Just as the wolf plunged into Little Red Creek, my horse, Sam Bass, hit the water and fell. (A horse will fall nearly every time if he hits water at too high speed.) I had my feet out of the stirrups and was thrown clear. I got a good ducking, the water being about four feet deep.

I was almost on top of the wolf when I fell, and when I came up I made a grab, landing the wolf quickly.

The President stopped his horse and, as I came out, he exclaimed:

"That shows the difference between man and dog in water with a wolf. Abernathy, I believe it is

117

easier for you to catch a wolf in water than on land, but it does not seem to bother you in either place."

If it seemed easy, that was largely due to my horse and dog. Few people who have not had experience in handling domestic animals can realize the amount of intelligent understanding and the almost human confidence and courage and affection with which they will enter into trying service that makes possible an almost perfect team-work between man and brute. The truth of this assertion was never better exemplified than in the fidelity, skill, and never-failing courage of Sam Bass, the gray racing horse, whom I preferred to ride to all others in wolf catching; and of the little blue greyhound bitch,[1] both of whom are so frequently mentioned in this book. If ever any human being had perfect understanding and perfect coöperation in action from comrades and friends that ran on four feet, I had it from these two. After the first few times that each had been taken out for a wolf hunt, I never began to saddle up for such a purpose that each, in its own way, did not give every evidence of pleasure at the prospect. That I always had sympathetic understanding from these animal friends scarcely needs to be stated; yet, best of all, they understood me and each other perfectly. It made possible team-work in which neither man, horse, nor dog ever failed or disappointed either of the other actors in the scene.

President Roosevelt, himself noted for his sympathetic interest in and understanding of all animate creation, seemed to sense and appreciate this unusual coördination of understanding and action of

---

[1] This bitch was poisoned, together with eleven of my other greyhounds, at Guthrie, three years later.

horse and hound with the rider who was directing the chase.

In this connection, also, let the reader recall that it was the courage and fidelity of a greyhound that made it possible for me to catch and hold captive my first wild wolf, in the days of my early youth, more than a dozen years before.

At the camp fire that night, the President was asking what had been my most dangerous catch and I told him the following tale:

"It was about four weeks ago, Mr. President, that I came over here in a wagon with a trailer hitched on behind containing a wolf cage. I brought Mrs. Abernathy and the five children with me; also Jim Wylie, my nephew. After five days I had caught only thirteen wolves. I decided that my family had had enough of camping for a while, and planned to take them back home Friday.

"Just as we were ready to leave, early Friday morning, I said to my wife,

" 'I am going to take the two little dogs, drop south a half-mile, and capture one more wolf. I don't like to leave on Friday with thirteen wolves.'

"I left instructions with Mrs. Abernathy that when she saw me wave my hat, she should send for Jim Wylie to help me. I told her to stay right where she was with the children.

"About three-quarters of a mile from the wagon I located three wolves. I took off my hat and waved, and we were off for the race. I was riding Sam Bass and had the two dogs. Going over a hill to the south, the wolves hit a draw that led back north. Had my wife kept driving, she could have seen me and possibly saved me from danger, but she stayed where I had left her. The wolves kept running up the draw, crossing the old road that we were to cross later in the wagon. Just as I crossed the road, Sam Bass hit one of the dogs, killing it instantly, and falling himself. Fortunately, he went only to his knees, and I was not thrown.

"When we got straight again, my little blue bitch was running neck and neck with one wolf. I ran right up beside them, begging her to take hold, but she kept looking back for the dog which my horse had killed.

"I was riding for dear life, and just as we went out on smooth ground, I leaped from my horse, almost rolling over both the dog and wolf. They snapped at each other and fell. I made a quick leap to the left and seized the wolf, at the same time leaping astride him. My horse went on as hard as it could go.

"Things were certainly not going as they should. Just then, the second wolf ran in and snapped me through the glove on the right hand a half-dozen times, apparently trying to force me to free its mate.

"I yelled, hallooed, and kicked with my foot that was free. I reached into the left pocket of my pants and found my knife, opened it with my teeth, and, as the second wolf attacked me again, I cut a six-inch gash in the shoulder, breaking off the short hawl-bill blade. The blade remained in the wolf's gaping wound, and the blood streamed. The wolf backed off about ten feet and crouched upon the ground.

"To my left I noticed a third wolf, crouching, ready to spring on me. I thought to myself, 'If this wolf attacks me, I am a goner for keeps.'

"My little dog was on the ground back of me, panting for dear life. She was frightened and I didn't blame her—so was I. I could not fight this third wolf.

"I started for the top of the hill, carrying the first wolf in my arms. (This hill was the highest point around there.) When I reached the top, I was startled to see a herd of four or five hundred head of 'jingle-bob' steers that Tom Waggoner had just shipped into the pasture from New Mexico. These steers were of the wildest kind, and would even fight a man on a horse. When they saw me with the wolf in my arms, they lost no time in charging toward me. When they were within six feet, I fell down on top of the wolf, gripping the animal by the lower jaw and lying as close as possible to the ground. The steers bawled and pawed, the whole herd crowding around me. I could feel their warm breaths upon the back of my neck.

"As a last resort, I was ready, if necessary, to pry myself loose with my left hand from the wolf's jaw, which held my right hand securely. I planned to mount one of the steers by grabbing its horns, forcing it to carry me to safety. This seemed possible, since I had on spurs with the rowels tied. I could have sunk the rowels deep into the flesh and ridden anything. At least, I could have stampeded the herd.

"I must have been there surrounded by that herd for at least ten minutes (though to me it seemed like an eternity). During this time Jim Wylie had gone south quite a distance and then returned back to the wagon, having failed to locate us. He said to my wife,

" 'I believe Uncle Jack has run clear out of the country.'

"Mrs. Abernathy stood up on the dashboard and took a look around the country. She saw the big herd far to the west. Jumping down, she handed my six-shooter to Jim, saying,

" 'Jim, take this six-shooter. Go to that big herd over yonder in the west; your uncle Jack may be right inside that herd. Hurry!'

"I heard a pistol bark out six shots. The cattle jumped, broke and ran. When Jim reached me, I was lying there unhurt still holding my wolf. That, Mr. President, is about as close a call as I want to have."

"Abernathy," he said, "I want to go and see the identical spot where all this took place." Accordingly the next day, I took him over there. It was early in the morning before the riders started on the hunt.

"Abernathy, promise me that you never again will take a chance like that," said the President. "You have other work to do."

I continued to catch wolves for the President for the rest of the six-day entertainment. Then he invited me to accompany him to Colorado, where he was going to hunt big game for a few days. But I had to decline: I could not leave my family so long.

On the last day, the President asked to meet Mrs. Abernathy and the children, so I had them come out to the Big Pasture. They spent a very pleasant hour with the President. Later, this meeting meant much to my two boys—but a later chapter in this book tells that story.

CHAPTER XVI

CLEANING UP AFTER A WESTERN TORNADO

A few days after the close of the wolf hunt in the Big Pasture, I received a telegram from Governor Thompson B. Ferguson asking me, as U. S. Deputy Marshal of Oklahoma, to take charge of affairs in Snyder, Oklahoma, and remain on duty until the arrival of a detachment of the National Guards. I learned that on the night before (May 10, 1905) this three-year-old town of some fifteen hundred had been practically wiped out by a tornado.

Four or five years before, when the railroad townsite promoters first announced the location of the new junction, it was reported that Indians living near by had warned of danger from tornadoes. The Indians related how the air currents seemed to draw storms through the mountain pass. They pointed out that no trees existed in the path because of the storms, although along the outside there were very large trees with years of growth.

Riding Sam Bass, I arrived at Snyder during the early forenoon. I shall never forget the sight that I saw. I immediately organized a force of fifteen men to guard the town. Ghouls—the demons who rob the dead—did but little of their ungodly work at Snyder. However, within a few hours we filled the calaboose with men arrested for fighting, drunkenness, and thieving. Some of those arrested we had to send to Lawton for safe-keeping.

Of all the sickening sights I ever saw in my life, those at Snyder were the most pitiful. Perhaps the worst of all was the piles of dead—men, women, and children—placed in the morgue, which had formerly been a dry-goods store. The shelves and counters which formerly had held merchandise were now holding human bodies. The sight of the children killed, their little arms dangling from the shelves, was the most heart-breaking of all.

A temporary hospital was established in the hotel. Medical aid had been rushed up by freight cars from Frisco, Oklahoma. Physicians, nurses, and others who wished to help were brought in, but many came from pure curiosity. The hotel was one of the few remaining buildings in the business district. The roof leaked and every time the rain poured down (which it did for two days) water ran onto the patients. The streets were several inches deep in water. Eighty-six had lost their lives, and there were about one hundred and fifty wounded.

Only one cottage was left standing north of the railway station. The big brick roundhouse had been blown to pieces, brick being scattered over the ground hundreds of yards. Of six hotels in the town, only two were left erect. The Commercial, one of the hotels that was only damaged, caught fire after the storm, adding to the confusion.

Among the freaks of the storm, a baby was blown right out of its mother's arms and killed. A couple who had planned to be married that night had postponed their scheduled wedding until the next day. Both were killed. A man, during the excitement, grabbed a woman who he believed was his wife and ran to a dugout, hoping to escape the storm. They arrived safely. Then finding that he had saved another woman, he went back to look for his wife—only to find her body. One man was blown nearly a block, landing on the back of a horse. Two men, hands clasped, were found dead on the roof of a house, where the wind had blown them. Dismembered bodies and parts of bodies were found everywhere, some a mile from the town. I saw railroad tracks that had been twisted like lightning rods. I saw chickens with all their feathers blown off. I saw a wagon with every spoke blown out of the wheels, the hubs resting on the ground. (This wagon had been loaded with two tons of coal, all of which was still in the box.) Needle grass was blown into a post, the pressure being so great that the grass was forced into the post two to three inches. I watched a man dig some of it out. After seeing the things I did I shall hesitate to dispute any statements made about freaks that occur in tornadoes.

Touched by the horrors of this fearful visitation upon the unfortunate community, the people of Oklahoma subscribed liberally to the relief fund, and thus the work of reconstruction and rehabilitating the stricken town was soon under way.

As is usual under such circumstances, however, fear, even to the point of terror, seemed to have seized the minds and hearts of the people all over the state. Everywhere, for weeks afterward, people were busy digging storm caves.

CHAPTER XVII

CALLED TO WASHINGTON

The petty rivalry of which I had been the object during the course of the wolf hunt in the Big Pasture was but a small incident in comparison with the experience that was awaiting me when I was now unexpectedly drawn into public life as a result of my new friendship with President Roosevelt.

It all came about through local politics. From the first day of its settlement in 1889, Oklahoma had been over-supplied with ambitious politicians; in fact, in proportion to its population, it has always had more past-masters in politics than any state in the Union. Consequently, nothing quickened political activity more than the sudden appearance of a new face in the political arena. As a political factor I had been unknown. As a new-found friend of the President of the United States, I was regarded in political circles as an interloper and my appearance was resented.

Since Mr. Roosevelt was the organizer and ultimate commander of the famous Rough Rider regiment, many of whose officers and men were from Oklahoma, it was but natural for the veterans of that organization to exert a very positive influence with the President in matters pertaining to affairs of the territory. Even before I was projected into public notice, the old-line politicians of Oklahoma were noticeably jealous of any of the young Spanish-American war veterans who had belonged to the

President's own regiment and who were likely to become prominent in the public life of the Territory. The well-known loyalty of the President to his friends, and especially to those who had served with him in the army, was the occasion of much anxiety among the members of the "Old Guard" in Oklahoma Territory.

There was a disposition in many quarters to credit me with having induced the President to make his visit to Oklahoma, more especially since there had been a strong effort on the other side of the Red River to stage the event in northern Texas. Of course, Texas people were inclined to believe that, since I had been born and reared in Texas, I would readily agree that the hunt should be held there instead of in Oklahoma. But the place of my birth or my residence did not influence me. As I said before, I decided to stage the hunt on the open prairie, where there would be the least danger of injury to the President. The fact that I had won the friendship of the President in such a short time naturally aroused great popular interest. However, I did nothing to help this along, and asked the President for nothing. When the wolf hunt was ended, I returned to my family on the ranch. However, many of my good friends and neighbors were inclined to think that this opportunity should be capitalized politically, and they were not hesitant in expressing their opinions. Almost immediately some of them began to suggest to the Administration at Washington that I be appointed to a federal position. The newspapers, too, were friendly to the idea.

Of course I had a good acquaintance all over most of the three new counties—Comanche, Kiowa, and Caddo. I had a commission as a deputy under the United States Marshal, Bill Fossett. After the opening of the state, with its throngs of settlers and adventurers, there was much trouble as to the sale of whiskey to Indians. Not only did the hip-pocket bootleggers violate the federal law prohibiting the sale of liquor to the Indians, but many saloon keepers who held government and local licenses did the same thing on the sly. I had occasion to make a number of arrests among the Indians of the three tribes in the reservation, practically all of whom knew me. I am sure that I held the confidence and respect of most of them as well as the friendship of nearly all of them who knew me personally—except perhaps some of the law breakers.

I must interrupt my story to tell about one of these Indians—Post Oak Jim.

Comanche tribesmen received money through the Government, collected from ranchmen who leased grazing land. This cash was paid once a month. During pay days and pow-wows, the Indians would get drunk. It was then that I had most of my trouble with tribe members. Post Oak Jim, one of the worst of the Comanche tribe, led a crowd of more than a hundred braves to the jail at Cache, a small town, for the purpose of trying to liberate Tom Wrinkles. I had arrested Wrinkles on a charge of selling whiskey to the Indians during a Fourth of July celebration. Hearing about the big crowd of Indians at the jail, I rode over to see what the trouble was. Post Oak was sitting on his horse, giving orders in the Comanche tongue. I understood enough of the language to know that the tribesmen planned to overturn the small jail, knocking the bottom out. This was the easiest way, Post Oak said, to liberate Tom Wrinkles.

"Damn you!" shouted Post Oak Jim, as he looked at me.

Post Oak Jim was over six feet tall and weighed two hundred and thirty pounds. He was nearly twice my size but no match for me in strength. I leaped from the ground, catching Post Oak by the collar, dragging him off his spotted pony. He struck me as I held him. I then drew my six-shooter and Indians fled in every direction. I then placed Post Oak Jim behind the bars beside the man whom he had planned to liberate.

Politicians in Oklahoma, as well as patronage seekers in other parts of the United States, became peevish at President Roosevelt because many time-honored formalities had been abandoned, especially in the matter of official appointments. But Mr. Roosevelt was a believer in rewarding merit and in ignoring formalities. He did not listen to the pleas of party leaders in Oklahoma, at any rate in my case. He simply sent for me to come to see him.

Now, I did not have the ready cash to pay for the long trip to Washington. I was not so fortunate even as some newspaper men were in Territorial days. Editors had semi-annual passes over nearly all railroads. Some public officials likewise were provided with free passes, but I did not come in that class, since I was only a deputy in the U. S. Marshal's field force. I therefore went to a bank in Frederick, and borrowed cash enough for a ticket and my expenses. I left with eighty-seven dollars after paying for a round-trip ticket from Frederick to Washington. Upon reaching St. Louis, Mo., I still had eighty-four dollars left, all of which was in twenties except four dollars in silver.

Riding in a chair car all the way to St. Louis on a slow train from Oklahoma was very tiresome. I was seriously in need of sleep when I arrived there. My train from St. Louis did not leave for eight hours. A policeman directed me to a hotel near by, where I registered and paid for a room. Since I was myself an officer of the law, I did not dream but that the fellow officer was directing me to a safe place.

Before leaving the depot, I checked my baggage. At first I decided to leave the old-time, trusty six-shooter in one of my "grips." But before I walked away from the check room, I suddenly decided to take my gun—and a good thing I did.

Every newspaper, from the smallest country patent-sheet to the biggest metropolitan daily, had run stories about "Catch 'em Alive Jack"; consequently, when it became known that I was in the city, I was besieged by reporters and photographers. I knew that if I registered at a prominent hotel I should get no sleep, so I decided to go to a cheap place to avoid reporters.

When I reached the hotel suggested by the policeman, I was shown to a room and was soon in bed. My trousers, with the purse containing my money, were placed on a chair beside the bed. There were two doors in the rooms, one of them near the chair. This door appeared to be locked. I locked the other with a key. Dozing off quickly, I was soon sound asleep.

How long I had been asleep, I don't know, but

it surely wasn't long, when I was awakened by the noise of one of the doors opening. No one was in the room, but I was sure that the door which I had thought locked near the chair had closed. I jumped up, seized my pistol, and tried to open the door. It was locked.

I threw my shoulder against the door, and it swung open. Then things began to happen.

Behind that door was the worst looking old hag I ever saw. I grabbed her with one hand, holding my pistol in the other, jerking her into my room. She began screaming at the top of her voice. Her yells brought a man and woman running into the room through the front door. This man had a gun in his hand as he entered, but when I took the drop on him, I hurled the old woman between us, ordering him to drop his gun. He did.

"There's your damned old pocketbook," said the old woman as she threw it on the floor. I couldn't tell whether or not all of my money was inside the purse. (I didn't have time to look and wasn't thinking about the money during the fight.) I then forced all three of the robbers to back out of the door; then dressed hurriedly, and ran into the lobby of the hotel. All had fled from the building.

I counted my money and discovered that twenty dollars were missing from the purse. Upon meeting a policeman on the street as I left the hotel, I told him of the robbery.

"What kind of a town have you where a man is robbed in broad daylight?" I asked. "I was directed by your fellow officer to go to that hotel."

"You go up the front and I'll go up the alley— and we'll meet up there," replied the policeman.

"No, you go up the front and I'll go up the alley," I answered.

"You could not stop them," said he.

"You just think I can't," was my reply.

"Have you a gun?" asked the officer.

"Yes, sir, and a good one," I replied.

"What right have you to carry a gun?"

"Don't worry. I have a better right than you have."

I went up the alley, entering the hotel again from the back way, then going into the lobby. There was no one in the hotel except the Negro porter, who refused to talk. The policeman called me over to the corner of the room where the carpet was pulled up from the floor. A brand new section of floor had just been placed by a carpenter.

"The city got onto this place and discovered a trap door in this floor," said the officer. "The city forced them to take the door out. They may have another trap door. It is a good thing you woke up when you did, or maybe you would have waked up and maybe you wouldn't; you might not have known anything for a week or two."

I left the hotel, returning to the depot, where I remained till train time. I was worried over the loss of the money, fearing I would not have enough cash to make the trip to Washington and return.

Soon after the train left the Union Station, I met W. B. Johnson of Ardmore, district attorney for the Southern District of Indian Territory. Senator Chester I. Long of Kansas was with him. Both were on their way to Washington. I told them that I was likewise Washington bound to see the President. Both offered to help me arrange for an appointment with the President.

"It will be Cabinet day when we get there," said Senator Long. "Nobody is able to see the President on the day he meets the Cabinet. I doubt if it will be possible for you to see him for at least a week."

I registered at the Raleigh Hotel upon my arrival in Washington. I counted my money and decided that I did not have enough to remain in Washington for a week. So I ignored the suggestion made by Senator Long and Attorney Johnson, and went out at once to look for the White House. My two friends were in the same hotel, but they did not know that I had left so early that morning. I went along Pennsylvania Avenue, looking at the many buildings. From photographs I had seen I soon recognized the Capitol at the far end of the Avenue. Then my eyes fell upon a tall white building near at hand.

"This is the White House," I said to myself. I entered the front door, but to my surprise, I did not see any one who even looked like the President. I guess I had a kind of a fool notion that he would be there to meet me.

"I am looking for the President," I said to an usher.

"This is not where the President lives, cowboy," said he. That made me mad and I was about ready to take the usher on for a round or two, when a man in uniform offered to direct me.

"If you will go with me, I will show you the way," he said, and going out front, he pointed to the White House, a short distance away, saying:

"There it is, but you cannot see the President to-day—this is Cabinet day."

I made up my mind that I would not take "no" for an answer, so I went ahead. I was attired in a gray suit, with cowboy pants. The legs of my trousers covered my boot-tops. I wore my usual broad-brimmed white hat and doubtless had every appearance of a westerner. I walked through the iron gate, reaching the inside of the grounds, walked around until I saw a door to the executive offices, and went in.

I did not know at the time that I was violating the rules by entering the executive offices carrying a six-shooter. Had the Secret Service men known this, I possibly would have been thrown in jail without ceremony. An usher inside asked me for a card.

"I don't carry cards," I replied. Then a blank card was produced. I wrote my name upon the card and it was sent to the inside office. Upon the usher's return, I was told to follow, and we went into the office of Private Secretary William Loeb, Jr. The usher introduced me to Mr. Loeb.

"I know you, Mr. Abernathy," said the Secretary. "The President has told me so much about you that I know you without an introduction," he added. "The President will be delighted to see you; just go in that room, and we will talk later."

I entered the room, in which was a long table. Around the table there were a number of men seated. All of those present seemed to be solemn and unsociable. None of them offered to speak.

"Well, there are more real manners in a cow camp than in here," I thought to myself as I stood there holding my cowboy hat; I said nothing to them, however.

I felt like a signboard when none of the men offered me a seat. I looked around and saw a vacant chair at the head of the table. I decided to sit down in it and make myself at home. As I sat down, a smile appeared on the faces of all those men. This made me feel angry, for I thought they were making fun of me. I looked at them, I guess, as viciously as I ever looked at a wild wolf. I had first placed my hat on the table; but when they smiled I was so mad that I threw the hat into a corner.

I began to notice that there were names under the glass top of the table, in front of each man. It began to dawn on me that I was in the wrong place—that I was "up against it properly"—when suddenly I heard a door open back of me. Before I could look up, I recognized the President's voice.

"Good morning, gentlemen," said the President, as he began shaking hands with all of those present. He didn't notice me sitting at the head of the table. Suddenly he saw me.

"Oh, Wolfer!" he shouted. He started toward me. I began to realize that I was in the right church but in the wrong pew, and I started to get up out of the chair.

"You are getting mighty high up in the world, sitting in the President's chair at a Cabinet meeting," remarked the President, as I again started to get up.

"Let me out of here," I said, "I feel just like a rat in a corn crib," and all of the Cabinet members and the President laughed. But I didn't mind this laugh: it was friendly.

"Now, gentlemen, excuse me for a few minutes," said the genial Teddy, as he escorted me into his private office. "How are Mrs. Abernathy and the children?" he continued, and proceeded to call each of my five children by their first names, although he had seen them only once.

Reaching under a table, he presented me with a book entitled: *Outdoor Pastimes of an American Hunter,* which includes the story of the wolf hunt.

"Here is a book from the author to you," he said, and showed me that he had autographed it for me. "I want you to have dinner with me today," he continued.

I thought he meant the noon-day meal, and told him that since it was already eleven o'clock, I should not have time to go to my hotel and dress in time.

"I mean dinner at six o'clock," he continued, and I said,

"Oh, you mean my old supper time." He laughed and said,

"And my old supper time, too."

He then took me back to the Cabinet room and said:

"Gentlemen, I want you to know John R. Abernathy, the man who entertained me better than any President was ever entertained—by catching wild, ferocious wolves with his hands."

Immediately each of the Cabinet members, as he shook my hand, was so changed in his manner toward mc that I thought of Dr. Jekyll and Mr. Hyde.

I left the executive offices, returning to my room in the Raleigh Hotel. I again met Senator Long and Attorney Johnson.

"We were just fixing to drag the town, thinking you were lost," said the Senator. "Have you been out buying something already this morning?"

"No. The President *gave* me this," I replied, as I showed them the book. They looked at each other, and Long remarked,

"Johnson, do you know how I feel?"

"No, but I know what I am!" replied Johnson, after learning that I had seen the President at the Cabinet meeting.

"And that isn't all, gentlemen," I added, "I am going to chew with him tonight at six o'clock."

After this first trip to the White House, I felt perfectly at ease. The President invited me to come and go whenever I pleased, making the White House my home while in Washington. I lived there until I was ready to go home. At the dinner table one night the President said,

"What would you like in Oklahoma, Jack?"

"I really don't know, Mr. President. I would not accept anything that I was not capable of taking care of."

"From the judgment you exhibited and the way everything was taken care of on the wolf hunt, I do not believe there is anything within my gift that you could not take care of."

"That is a compliment, Mr. President, that I shall never forget. I am afraid that you are making that a little strong, however."

"How would you like to be United States Marshal of Oklahoma?" he asked.

"That would be a very important position. I would do my best to carry out the law to the letter."

"That's fine," said he. No more was said about this during my first trip. I started home next day.

About a month later, the President sent me a telegram asking me to return to Washington at once.

I made the trip, arriving during the early part of the week. My name already had been sent to the Senate for confirmation as Marshal of Oklahoma. The Senate was to act on the confirmation on the following Tuesday.

"Did Dennis Flynn sign your recommendation?" Teddy asked me when I again saw him.

"No, Mr. President, Dennis said my recommendation was a blanket endorsement; that he wouldn't endorse me."

"Well, Dennis is a good fellow, but—" and that was all the President said.

Mr. Flynn had been delegate to Congress for many years. Then, as today, members of Congress nearly always are consulted by the President in making appointments.

The President asked me to call upon the Senate Judiciary Committee on the following Monday morning. I asked the President what he wanted me to say to the Committee members, and he laughed heartily.

"This is one time that every tub must stand upon its own bottom," he replied. He handed me a package of telegrams clamped in book form, which he told me to read. He suggested that this would put me in position to know what to talk about.

Charges had been preferred against me, and I was asked to answer them before the committee. The charges read something like this:

"John Abernathy has been a bronco rider and a wolf catcher; was reared in a cow camp; has been a fiddler at country dances, a cotton picker, a patch digger, and a friend of the outlaws—and is not a politician." Other charges were that "He would appoint Al Jennings, notorious ex-outlaw as his chief deputy, and Simon Dalton, youngest brother of the Dalton Brothers (killed in the Coffeyville raid) as his federal jailer." (Of course, these last two charges were not true.)

A delegation of twelve or fifteen men, Republicans from Oklahoma, called on the President and asked for an interview. They were told to wait half an hour. Some one whom I knew was present when the delegation talked to the President and told me the following:

"The President came into the room. After members of the delegation had been introduced to him and greeted him very informally, the President seated himself on a big flat-top desk in the center of the room, and thus addressed the men:

" 'Gentlemen, I take it that you have called to see me for the purpose of filing protests against the appointment of John Abernathy as United States Marshal of Oklahoma.' When all nodded in the affirmative, he continued,

" 'Well, in that event, I will listen to all that you have to present or say, but I want you to know that I will appoint Mr. Abernathy to the position, regardless of any representations that you may have to make.' "

I did not have much trouble in explaining to the Senate Judiciary Committee when I appeared. Senator Knox said,

"It would seem that some of your Oklahoma friends do not think you would be a fit man for U. S. Marshal; I'll just have the secretary read the charges."

The committee had been furnished a copy of

each telegram and I had read them all. One of the Senators told me it cost about thirteen hundred dollars to send all of the telegrams from Oklahoma which protested my appointment. There was a stack of telegrams about six inches thick.

"I will tell you the part of the charges that are not true; then you will know the truthful part," I said. "The last three statements are not true. I would be as far from appointing Al Jennings or Simon Dalton to any office under me as any of you gentlemen would be if you were in my place. However, I know both Al and Frank Jennings. We are friends. They once were bad men, but have reformed and are trying to live right. According to the Scripture, 'There is more rejoicing among the angels in Heaven over one sinner that repenteth than there is over ninety and nine righteous men that need no repentance.' "

"Well, if you were reared in a cow camp, where did you get all that Scripture?" asked one of the Senators.

"Senator, I thought that everybody knew that verse."

"You are a fiddler for country dances?"

"Yes, sir. And there never was a dance broken up in a row where I furnished the music."

"How do you account for that? Were they afraid of you?"

"No, sir. But I was the only fiddler on the Plains at that time. If a row started, I told them I would get scared and quit. That is how I kept peace and order."

I noticed a smile at that, and Senator Knox leaned back in his chair, saying:

"Well, Marshal—I am going to call you Marshal, since your name already has gone to the Senate—tell us some wolf stories."

I told them two stories, and when I started to make my exit, one of the Senators said:

"Don't go yet. Tell us some more. I could listen a dry week if it rained every day, to such stories as those."

It took three attempts before I finally got away and returned to my hotel. I had been there only a few minutes, when I got a phone call. It was from Secretary Loeb, wanting me to come to the White House at once. I lost no time in getting to the President.

"I want to know what you did to those Senators?" he said. "Every man jack of them has called me and they have said some pretty good things about you, too."

Thus I became Marshal of Oklahoma. The position was one of great responsibility and trust. The salary was five thousand dollars a year (a big sum to me), and all expenses incurred while in the discharge of duty.

My appointment meant moving my family from the west part of Comanche (now Tillman) to the capital, then at Guthrie. It was a great event, especially to my children. Of course I took all my dogs and my horse, Sam Bass. I could not part from them.

About a year after we moved, my wife died and I was left with six children. (I am happy to say that I was able to bring all of them up safely, and that they are all alive today.)

CHAPTER XVIII

I AM A GUEST IN THE WHITE HOUSE

While I was a guest at the White House I went with the President nearly every morning for his usual early morning walk. He was such a rapid walker that I was always tired out after one of our tramps in and around the city.

One cold, crisp morning we went for a walk along Rock Creek, about three miles north-west of the White House. When we reached the water he did not seem to notice it: he waded in nearly waist deep without saying a word. I did not like the idea of plunging into that water on such a cold morning. My blood was none too thick, for I was not accustomed to the cold air of the North, and when I hit the water I was so chilled that my teeth almost rattled. However, I followed the President.

I was carrying two pistols at the time, one on my hip and the other under my arm. I took the one pistol off my hip and held it above my head so that it wouldn't get wet, but I left the other in the scabbard, where it got well soaked. We walked down along the creek about a quarter of a mile, then recrossed it, wading as before; but the water was not so deep. Returning to the White House, we changed clothes and suffered no ill effects. The President did not seem to be at all exhausted from the long hike, and I told him he could outwalk a camel if he would exercise like that for awhile. However, I was very tired and glad to get back. I was more used to a saddle.

This was just a small illustration of the President's nature: he was afraid of nothing. His was a fighting disposition—brave, but not overbearing. He was hard on himself, but was kind to those who were in distress, and always anxious to help the underdog. During our wolf chases if anything happened to a man, horse, or dog, he was the first to dismount and offer to give aid.

After we returned from Rock Creek that cold morning the Roosevelt boys—Theodore, Jr., and Archibald—and the younger children were having a circus on roller skates in front of the White House. The President and Mrs. Roosevelt—a wonderful mother—allowed the children to have every healthful liberty.   Miss Alice, the oldest, was an attractive girl with a disposition very much like her father's. The home life of the Roosevelts was very much like that of the average American family, and they were just like regular home folks to their friends and visitors.

I was greatly impressed by the President's firmness one day when Senator Shelby M. Cullom of Illinois appeared at the executive offices for a conference.   The Senator was in company with the father of a young man in the United States Navy. The father had appealed to the Senator in an effort to secure a cancellation of the boy's enlistment. The youth's mother was dying, the President was told.   Both the father of the youth and the Senator made tearful pleas for release of the young man.   I observed the President very closely as the pitiful pleas were made, and noticed him as his face became serious and his jaws set.

"Senator," he said, "I cannot do what you request.

There was one President who started to grant a request like this—on a plea of a "dying mother"—and it almost broke up the Navy. There was such a flood of appeals—so many mothers were dying—that it would have been impossible to keep the Navy in operation had all the requests been granted. There comes a time in the life of every young man who enlists when he gladly would be willing to give a right arm to secure a release, but that desire soon passes."

The President continued to talk about the young men in the Navy, declaring that he understood their difficulties, having been in close contact with the service while Secretary of War.

"Mr. President, you are right," replied the father of the youth, as he grasped the hand of the Chief Executive; and in company with the Senator he then left the office.

"I could not have turned down that old man; if I was mentally able to take care of this office I would not be physically able," was my comment on the father's plea.

"Well, Jack," replied the President, laughing, "you are a pretty good man physically—for I have not forgotten the time you knocked me down when we were boxing."

President Roosevelt and I had often put on the gloves for sparring bouts, for he enjoyed such athletic stunts. Boxing, as he had learned in the days of youth, kept him in first-class physical trim. We always boxed about one round and then rested for a few seconds. On one occasion the President walked over to the center of the ring and asked,

"Jack, are you doing your best?"

"Yes," I replied, though I really did not feel like doing my best that morning.

"I would not like you so well, if I thought you were not," he continued.

"Do you really mean that?"

"I surely do."

A crowd of the President's friends were watching us. About the third time we came together after the gong sounded, I knocked the President into the ropes. He came back at me with several hard punches and it was with no little difficulty I managed to protect myself. In boxing, President Roosevelt practiced the psychology of his life—when he hit, he hit hard.

I remember that it was three years after Senator Cullom had tried to induce the President to release the son of a "dying mother" from the Navy, when I attended a reception given in the White House. The President was seated beside Andrew Carnegie. When I walked in, the former arose, saying:

"Jack, who do you think was here to see me yesterday?"

"I don't know."

"It was the 'dying mother' you scolded me about for refusing to let her son out of the Navy. She held my hand and thanked me a dozen times, saying, 'Your action made a man out of my son—he has been offered a promotion and expects to re-enlist in the Navy.' "

By the time I had got well into my Marshal's job I had been called to Washington several times in order to answer the charges lodged by my political opponents, so that when I got a message to appear before the President I naturally felt sure it was for the purpose of defending myself against further accusations. Under the policy of the federal rule, when charges of any nature are brought against an official, the Department of Justice immediately sends an inspector to make the probe. This inspector usually is a total stranger to the official. All persons who have statements to make are questioned. Signed statements are made under oath and recorded with a copy of the charge. An answer then is made by the accused official. In this instance, Secretary W. M. Loeb, Jr., had sent a telegram to me at Guthrie, which was as follows:

"The President wishes you to be in Washington Wednesday."

I had been in Guthrie less than a month since appearing before the Department of Justice. "More charges," I commented to Chris Madsen, chief deputy. I departed for Washington immediately.

I walked into the Executive Office on Tuesday morning, a day ahead of their requested time, and after shaking hands with the President, I said,

"I did not expect more charges so soon."

"Did you come all the way from Oklahoma thinking you were to answer more charges?" he replied.

"Yes." Then, to my surprise, he said,

"I do not think there will be any more charges for awhile. Wednesday night I am going to entertain my classmates who finished with me at Harvard, and I could not think of a man better able to entertain them than you—so I wired you to come."

For once in my life I realized my limitations when I thought of making an appearance as a speaker before those highly cultured friends of the President.

"Don't you think you have made a mistake, Mr. President?" I asked, as I thought about my predicament.

"No, sir! No, sir!" he replied.

"I had much rather you had said, 'I have thirteen outlaws out here near the city; I want you to go single-handed and get them' than to have you ask me to entertain your college classmates," I said.

"Well, it will be all right," he assured me, slapping me on the shoulder.

I slept very little that night. I was thinking of and dreading that entertainment. The next morning I said to myself,

"Here goes nothing bound for nowhere."

I appeared before the assembled classmates, and I want to say that I never met a finer lot of men. As I recall it, there were thirty-two present. I entertained those men for an hour and a half, telling stories about catching wolves with my hands, my "bronc" riding, and other incidents of life on the frontier. When they shook hands as I finished, a number gave me cordial invitations to visit them at their homes.

Some of the stories I told are to be found in this book. When I told of hunts where the President was with me, I described the part that he took. After I finished speaking, the President talked, telling what he had seen me do. This occasion that I had dreaded turned out to be one of the most pleasant evenings of my life. And, best of all, I was able to think that I had pleased the President. Undoubtedly I made plenty of grammatical errors in telling my stories to those distinguished college men, but they seemed too interested to notice them.

In my recollections of meeting members of the
President's family, there comes to mind an interview
with Archibald, one of the younger sons, which took
place during the oil boom at Wichita Falls, Texas,
in 1919. He was employed by the Sinclair Oil Company. I was in Fort Worth on business at the time
I was informed that Archibald was at Wichita Falls.
I immediately went to see him. We had a delightful
visit, and he disclosed to me the details of his father's
last illness, and the struggle the Roosevelt boys had
in order to enter the World War. In telling of his
father's death, Archie said,

"Father never recovered from his hunting trip
in the tropics of South America. He contracted a
fever during that expedition from which he did not
wholly recover. The trip was the worst of all in
undermining his health. Then, too, the death of
Quentin, who was shot down in an airplane by the
Germans, had a great deal to do with father's break-
down, combined with disappointments over the Administration policies in handling the World War."

In after years, discussing President Roosevelt's
personal friendship for me, a federal judge and two
prominent attorneys gave me their opinion. One
of the attorneys said he thought it was because I had
a large family. The other said he thought it was
because of my determination and readiness for positive action. The judge declared it was because of
dare-deviltry and my knowledge of animals, both
domestic and wild. Maybe each of them was right.
I only know that seldom in this old world has there
been such a friendship as ours.

CHAPTER XIX

MEETING FAMOUS MEN

When I first went to Washington at the invitation of President Roosevelt, I had little idea of the number and prominence of other people that I should meet on my two dozen or more visits that were to follow. I made a good start when I met the heads of the Cabinet, but that was only a start. While in the Executive Mansion that first time I was introduced by Secretary Loeb to Mark Twain. Subsequently I met the noted humorist upon several other occasions, generally in New York City. Although I made no pretensions as a conversationalist—and do not now, for that matter—I did not need much initiative in a talk with the aging author of *Innocents Abroad:* he had plenty to say and was quite willing to do most of the talking.

In the course of subsequent visits to Washington, my circle of acquaintances in the official life of the Capital—civil, military, naval, legislative, judicial—was greatly extended. With it also came introductions to some of the greatest Americans in private life. Among these, in addition to Mark Twain, were Andrew Carnegie, Thomas A. Edison, and Alexander Graham Bell, all of whom I met in the White House.

Mr. Carnegie immediately displayed a keen interest in me, informing me that he had been partially reared on Abernathy's Biscuit, a well-known brand of bakery products in Scotland. His interest in me

149

was doubtless due in part to the Scottish origin of the Abernathy family, regarding the history of which he seemed to have some knowledge, including the story of the thirteen exiles who came to America in the beginning of the eighteenth century. Mr. Carnegie was present as one of the most interested observers in the White House when some of my moving pictures of wolf hunts were shown on the screen. Afterward I was a guest several times in Mr. Carnegie's New York home. We were never at a loss for conversation.

Mr. Edison was not so talkative as Mr. Carnegie, being of a more reflective turn of mind; but he was a splendid listener. Although invited to be a guest in Mr. Edison's home, I was never able to stay East long enough to visit him. However, I dined with him a number of times, always meeting him at the Waldorf Astoria Hotel. He seemed to be especially interested in asking about my hunting experiences, and also about my adventures as a peace officer.

At the Waldorf Astoria I also met Col. John Jacob Astor, who afterward went down on the Titanic in 1912.

Along with public officials and dignitaries in Washington, I also met many members of the Diplomatic Corps and other representatives of foreign nations. Among all of these, the one best remembered is the Ambassador of the French Republic, Monsieur Jean A. A. J. Jusserand, whose term of service in that capacity in Washington had already extended over a decade. Ambassador Jusserand seemed never to tire of talking with me about my life in the wilderness, with its dangers and excitements. At any time or place that I might be announced to speak, there the Ambassador was sure to show up as an interested listener. William Loeb, Jr., Secretary to President Roosevelt, once told me that he regarded the Ambassador from France as the best educated man in Washington, bar none. With all this, he was also a man of simplicity and sincerity, a delightful personality, and had a charm of manner that won all who came in contact with him.

Doctor Alexander Graham Bell, the inventor of the telephone, was one of the most noted men of his time. Aside from his business, he was interested in many other things, especially in science. I always found him to be very friendly, but I did not have opportunity to become as well acquainted with him as I did with the others I have mentioned.

I met Col. William F. Cody (Buffalo Bill) many times and in different places, and we became very warm friends. Cody had about as extensive an acquaintance as any man that ever lived and his ability to recognize faces and remember names was nothing short of marvellous. These traits, with his magnetic personality and his courteous consideration for all with whom he came in contact, won him a legion of friends. He invited me to join his Wild West Show, but I had other plans in view.

Another noted man, whom I did not meet at the White House, but with whom I came into terms of very warm friendship in New York, was O. Henry, the famous story writer, whose real name was Sidney Porter. Among my many friends, I liked none more than O. Henry.

In New York City I also met Franklin D. Roosevelt, then an ambitious young attorney, who had but recently married a niece of his distant cousin,

President Roosevelt.   The world had not heard much
of him then.

During the course of a reception at the White
House, President Roosevelt also introduced me to
Jack London.   London proved to be very jovial and
a good entertainer.   Subsequently, I met him in
New York several times.

I also met Irvin Cobb at the White House.   Mr.
Cobb, whom I afterward met a number of times in
New York, became very friendly.   After a time he
became quite insistent that he write my biography,
and he was quite surprised when I declined the
honor, on the ground that I was too young.

In New York City, I also met Bob Davis, well
known as a sporting man and magazine writer.   As
far as possible, Bob insisted that once each week I
should accompany him to see a prize fight, even
though it was not always convenient for me to do so.
He was mightily interested in the stories of my wolf
catching.   He asked me if I would be willing to fight
it out with a large and ferocious wolf if we were
locked inside a heavy steel cage.   I told him I sure
would.

Bat Masterson, another all-round sporting man,
magazine writer, and former peace officer at Dodge
City in the palmy days of the cattle trail, also became
an acquaintance of mine.   Though he had long
been a voluntary exile from the Plains, Bat's spirit
seemed to hark back to the days of his own young
manhood, when I, as a youngster from Oklahoma and
Texas, had been with him.   He loved to live the old
days over again.

Another friend of those days was Frank James,

once dreaded as a Missouri bandit, who had made his peace with the law and had traveled only the highway of peace for more than a quarter of a century. Of course, I met him only in the West, for he seldom if ever went East. In those days he had a horse ranch in south-western Oklahoma. Though no one ever offered to molest him, the long years when he was an outlaw, scouting and in hiding, had left their indelible mark upon him.

He was a brave man, yet he was always nervous and apprehensive. As an instance of this, he once asked me to unload and dismantle my six-shooter while we were together for a time. At that time he was following the racing circuits. When I attended the races with him, in Kansas City, my opinion concerning James then was that he either had straight tips as to winners or else he was a marvellous judge of horses; he seemed to cash in on nearly every wager that he made. Although he did not drink to excess, I noticed that two or three drinks made him quite talkative. On such occasions he would regale his friends by the hour with stories of his early adventures and exploits.

I shall never forget one night that James spent with me. He told me how, during the Civil War, soldiers had fired on his mother, shattering her arm; how his little half-brother had been killed; how their homestead had been burned and all of their livestock driven away, while he and Jesse had been with Quantrell's band of guerillas. When Frank and Jesse returned home, they learned of the tragedy, and when their mother told her story, he said that he and Jesse exchanged glances, kissed her, and then started for the door.

"Mother placed her uninjured arm around Jesse's neck, leaning against me as we walked toward the front door," Frank said. "On reaching the door the mother exclaimed: 'Boys! Boys! Don't do what you have made up your minds to do!'" Frank said they did not answer her, but just kissed her again, and left. Within forty-eight hours, Frank said, they had captured at least one-half of the soldiers who took part in the wounding of their mother and burning of the family home.

Before we went to bed that night, Frank said,

"Marshal, what kind of guns are those you are carrying?" I told him that the gun which I carried on my right hip was a German-made automatic with nine high-powered cartridges in the magazine and one in the barrel. This pistol had power enough to shoot through a railroad rail. Then I exhibited the .38-calibre pistol of the cowboy type which I carried in a holster under my left arm.

"That's a regular outlaw type," remarked Frank, as he noticed how easy it was to quickly make a draw from this leather scabbard. I said in reply,

"I have to compete with outlaws; why shouldn't I have an outlaw outfit?" Frank seemed surprised as I demonstrated to him how quickly I could make a draw with this six-shooter. This pistol was held in place by a wire spring which fastened around the barrel. Only a slight touch was necessary in drawing this gun. I had taken this improvised holster from an outlaw.

"Can you take that gun to pieces?" asked Frank. He began to inspect the German-made automatic. I took the magazine out, throwing the cartridges out of the barrel, then handed the pistol to him. "I mean, can you take that gun all to pieces?" continued Frank.   I went ahead and dismantled it.

"Now just leave it that way; you might be dreaming tonight that you were sleeping with an outlaw and get up and kill me!"

"Well, Frank," I said, "*that* corroborates the story I have often heard about you—you are like a wild turkey, always with your head up and looking for something."

"Well, you see I am here, don't you, and the others are all gone." He referred to other members of the James gang, most of whom had died with their boots on.

I discussed with Frank that night the different kinds of guns used by officers and outlaws.   Frank seemed to be an expert on guns.   He knew every detail about firing a six-shooter, especially the cowboy pistols.   But he had never used an automatic, he said.

When I first began riding the range, I quickly learned from older cowboys how to fire a six-shooter by "fanning the hammer."   In those early days, most of the officers and cowboys carried their guns on the right side, with the weapon seemingly backwards.   In making the draw, the right hand would go down with the wrist twisted.   The palm of the hand would be outward in grasping the pistol handle. In pulling the weapon from the scabbard upward, the right hand turns the weapon, the thumb cocking the pistol as the "drop" is being taken on the man.   Many of the old-time cowboys, in order to shoot their pistols rapidly, would file off the trigger entirely, using only the hammer, which they fanned either with the right thumb or the left hand while holding the pistol in the right.

I also soon discovered, however, that the most accurate way to fire a pistol is by holding the weapon with both hands. When this is done, pulling the trigger does not throw the gun out of line after aim is taken. Frank James agreed with me on this point.

"This automatic is my favorite gun," I told the ex-outlaw. "I prefer it as an officer in search of desperate men, also for hunting game birds or deer. I have killed a number of deer with this automatic; I've also shot many quail in the head with it."

We talked about the people I had arrested. I told him that I had arrested all types. Some were low bandits; others were of the intellectual type. I had arrested a Governor of the state, and even Carrie Nation.

CHAPTER XX

MARSHAL IN OKLAHOMA

Before I had been appointed as Marshal of the State of Oklahoma, I had tried to enlist in the army at the time Roosevelt was organizing the cavalry regiment for service in Cuba. I had appeared before the recruiting officer at Dallas. When he examined me, the physician told me that I was afflicted with organic heart trouble.

"You are an organic liar," I shouted, in anger. "I have broken bucking horses, have caught wolves, and have been in many fights; but my heart has never bothered me."

However, with the strong personal friendship of the President, I did not have to be a Rough Rider to secure my appointment as Marshal of Oklahoma Territory.

A total of 1,052 men applied for appointment in my office, or as field deputies. Each applicant was endorsed by from three to ten persons, many of them locally prominent.

I was the youngest Marshal ever appointed in the United States and at first I felt a certain delicacy in giving orders. I tried to give them in as few words as possible but always to the point. My requirements were: that no man should get drunk, or gamble in a resort; that he should not be without a six-shooter in hunting men; that he should use it only as a last resort in order to make an arrest; and that he should live up to the oath of office as the law demanded.

Inside of three months after I was sworn in as Marshal, as I have already told, charges were filed by Oklahoma politicians with President Roosevelt seeking to bring about my removal from office. My biggest job during the first term of office was to go to Washington every few months and answer charges filed against me. Although these trips strained my purse, I always was glad to go. It gave me a chance to visit the best friend I ever had—the President.

The fight for the judgeship of the Western District Federal Court in Oklahoma was very bitter. I possibly had more to do with the appointment of John H. Cotteral to the position than any other Oklahoman. (Cotteral was a neighbor of mine in Guthrie.)

I thought the President was joking with me when he said on one occasion: "Whom shall I appoint judge for Oklahoma in the Western District?"

"John Cotteral," I said. "He is a big, fine-looking fellow, and a good man for the place." The President turned, pushed a button, and, to my surprise, had Mr. Loeb, his secretary, send Cotteral's name to the Senate for confirmation.

I had also become a very close friend of George Garrison, sheriff of Oklahoma County. Garrison had been elected to a second term at the election. In the following spring, a Negro outlaw, Alf Hunter, alias Jim Kingsbury, terrorized the Negro district at Oklahoma City. This outlaw, while chasing his wife, shot down a poor helpless Negress, firing nine times into her body as she fell to the ground. Then he fled. Garrison trailed the fugitive murderer to a farm house near Hitchcock. Another Negro, acting as guide, took the sheriff and two peace officers to the place. Learning that the officers were after him, the renegade hid in the top of a haystack, whence he fired, killing Sheriff Garrison and wounding Deputy Fate Saunders. The officers returned the fire, a pitched battle taking place. Bullets from the officers' guns hit the Negro but failed to kill him. The slayer was later captured by Deputy Saunders; and was tried and hanged in the jailyard at Watonga. In the search for the outlaw, I took an active part.

Another spectacular affair with criminals took place soon after I became Marshal. Guthrie's historic old federal jail of stone, erected in pioneer days, was the scene of an attempted jail break. On that occasion, Sam Bass, my horse, made a real fast run for his master when I received a telephone call in my office one afternoon.

"Hole in the wall! Going to Hell!" was the only message I heard, as I took down the receiver. I recognized the voice as that of John Lankford, jailer. I did not wait to untie the reins which held Sam Bass. I slashed them and leaped into the saddle and Sam Bass was off.

R. A. Wright, convicted and under death sentence for murder of William Slattery, a farmer, was trying to liberate a total of 134 prisoners, many of them murderers and bandits. He was about halfway out of a hole that had been dug secretly in the rock wall.

"Get back!" I shouted, as I dashed up on Sam Bass, taking the drop on them with my six-shooter.

"Don't shoot!" pleaded Wright. "I can't get back." It was true; he was unable to work his way back inside the hole until some of the prisoners inside pulled him back by the legs.

One of my regular experiences as Marshal was to
duck bullets from bandits who "had it in for me."
On the occasion I am about to describe, my life was
saved by the intelligence of my faithful dog, Catch.

I had just moved to a rural home a mile and a
half south of Guthrie. One night Catch growled
and barked, acting as if he was trying to stop somebody at the front gate. I opened the front door.
As I did so, a pistol bullet whizzed by my head.
Three men were at the front gate. They broke and
ran west after firing the shot. A double hog-wire
fence was around the yard. The trio ran along the
outside of the fence, then fired another shot.

I was barefoot, but I ran out into the snow, empty-
ing my six-shooter at the fleeing men. I then returned inside, hurriedly put on my boots, and
grabbed my rifle and a flashlight. I then followed
the three for nearly a mile. One of the men I knew
was wounded, but I could not find them.

Three weeks later I was called to Harrah in order
to prevent a double bank robbery. (I had had a
tip from a woman whom I had befriended.) Chris
Madsen, chief deputy marshal, accompanied me on
the trip. We also took along a man by name of
Strubble and a posse of his choosing. Strubble and
the posse were stationed at one bank; Madsen and I
covered the other.

About twelve-thirty at night three men appeared
from the bank. I called on them to surrender, but
they opened fire on us. The first bandit to fall was
a man named Quigg. Carpenter, another bandit,
soon fell mortally wounded, but lived about twelve
hours. Dillbrook, the third member of the gang,
was believed to be fatally wounded when we took him

to the hospital, but he lived to serve a prison term. Carpenter said he knew the jig was up when he saw us there as they came out of the bank.

"I want to tell you," he said as I talked with him before he died, "you have the smartest dog on earth." He then admitted that it was he and two other men who had tried to assassinate me at my home.

Another plot was hatched out to murder me while I was living at this same place. A fund of fifteen hundred dollars had been subscribed to pay for the "job." Fred Hudson, outlaw and former member of the Bert Casey gang, was to kill both James Bourland and me. Hudson, who was the man that had killed Bert Casey and his outlaw partner, did not like me. Bourland, my field deputy stationed at Anadarko, learned the details of the plot during the trial of the Hughes brothers at Hobart. Bourland had arrested the Hughes brothers, old-time outlaws, in Washita County, charged with murder of a youth whose body was found upon their ranch. When Bourland learned of the murder plot, the day before the Hughes brothers were acquitted, he came to me at Guthrie, arriving at night. He told me of the plot.

"Now, Marshal, I believe I can handle a gun as well as anybody and I want to stay with you till the thing is over," he said.

I would not permit this, telling Jim that he was needed at Anadarko; that I had mailed him a bunch of papers to be served; that I was able to take care of myself. Bourland went back to Anadarko that night, and was killed the next morning. As long as I live, I shall regret that I did not allow him to remain with me as he wished.

On the day of the killing of Bourland, Hudson

started to Guthrie, where he had planned to kill me, then return to Anadarko and kill Bourland. After he arrived in Anadarko, on his way to Guthrie, he began to drink and soon became quite drunk. As he was armed and inclined to be quarrelsome, the situation called for attention. He was threatening to shoot an inoffensive man when Bourland appeared on the scene, disarmed him, and warned him to be quiet. Subsequently Hudson secured a gun and started hunting for Bourland. He found him in a saloon, and, without pausing to give warning, fired, inflicting a fatal wound. Despite the injury, Jim continued to stand up and return the fire, hitting Hudson in the knee. Both men fell. Bourland died the following morning and Hudson in the afternoon of the same day from blood poisoning. The wound was so bad that it had been necessary to amputate the leg.

One of my most interesting arrests was that of James Miller, ranchman from Pecos, Texas, who it was claimed was a professional killer of men. Miller was wanted for murder.

In making the arrest, the officers surrounded a residence where Miller's sister lived. He had been making his home with her. Miller was taken to Ardmore by my deputies. Later, he was taken by a mob and hanged in an old barn. Before he was executed, it is claimed that he confessed to the killing of a total of forty-nine men.

A reward of one thousand dollars had been offered for the capture of Miller. I never did receive that reward, but I still have hopes.

CHAPTER XXI

WOLVES IN THE WHITE HOUSE

While President, from September, 1901, until March, 1909, Theodore Roosevelt had in the White House nearly every kind of wild animal and reptile, either mounted or alive. There were even wild, snapping wolves—but they were only in moving pictures, which I made while on vacation in the Wichita Mountains of Oklahoma, in the summer of 1907. A moving picture taken in the U. S. Forest Reserve was shown twice—the first time for the President, his family, and friends; the second, for officials of the Government. Those who attended the showings included the Supreme Court Justices, their wives and children; members of the Cabinet and their families—in fact, the entire official family, more than six hundred people in all. Later, these pictures were shown before several thousand at the Army and Navy headquarters in Washington.

After staging the entertainment in honor of President Roosevelt, in the Big Pasture of Oklahoma in April of 1905, I had received many flattering proposals from theatrical organizations and cities throughout the nation, offering large sums of money if I would stage exhibitions of wolf catching. Among the many offers was one from Frank J. Bostick, animal king, inviting me to perform at Coney Island, New York. Bostick offered me $100,000 for such an exhibition, to be held at Coney Island.

Kansas City and St. Louis sent delegations to

Oklahoma, trying to induce me to appear before the public in those places. Realizing that it would not be proper to engage in such exhibitions, I wrote to President Roosevelt, telling him of the offers. In my letter I explained that I didn't want to stage any theatrical performances while holding a Government position; that, however, I wanted to be diplomatic with my friends in the East.

President Roosevelt, in reply to this inquiry, sent the following letter:

> THE WHITE HOUSE
>   Washington,
>   June 4, 1906.
>
> My Dear Marshal
>   I guess you had better not catch live wolves as a part of a public exhibition while you are Marshal.
>   If on a private hunt you catch them, that would be all right; but it would look too much as if you were going into the show business if you took part in a public celebration.
>   Give my regards to all your family. I am sure you are doing well in your position.
>   Sincerely yours,
>   THEODORE ROOSEVELT.
>
> Hon. John R. Abernathy
> United States Marshal,
> Guthrie, Oklahoma.

I sent copies of this letter from the President to the various committees.

A short time after the wolf hunt in the Big Pasture I first discussed with the President whether he believed it would be possible to secure a moving picture of a wolf hunt. He expressed the belief that it would be impossible to get moving pictures of such an event, but I decided to try it.

Hon. James Wilson, Secretary of Agriculture, gave permission in 1907 to make the moving pictures of the wolf catch on the Forest Reserve in the Wichita Mountains, and a complete camp from the Fort Sill Military Reservation was furnished. Four mule teams were used to haul the camp outfit up into the mountains. Our camp was near Blur Lake, adjoining Crater Dam, seven miles north of Cache. There were twenty-five men in the camp.

We went after loafer wolves on this trip. Our information was that a large number of big loafers would be found in that area. I used every effort to make a success of this event, since the pictures were to be shown before the Government officials. I found out, however, before this catch was over, that the wolves were about as smart as I was.

We killed a cow for bait, placing the meat at a point where we knew the wolves would be likely to travel. (Wolves will not touch bait till the scent of human hands leaves, which takes about twenty-four hours.)

The first wolf I caught came within twenty feet of the camera. The operator, however, got excited and spoiled the picture.

Perhaps the most exciting catch I made during this chase was the capture of a big loafer in water. Our outfit was about fifteen miles from headquarters camp, near Cache and close to Medicine Creek. It was about daylight and our moving-picture machines were located about two hundred yards apart. We were standing with our horses' heads together, talking.

Al Jennings, former outlaw; Bill Kirby, John Lankford, my federal jailer; Sim Shepherd, police chief of Lawton; and a number of others were with me. We did not think there was anybody else within miles of us. Suddenly a man rode up toward us from the north, on one of the prettiest sorrel horses I ever looked at in my life. He was dressed neatly and appeared to be about twenty-four years old.

On the previous day, Al Jennings had ridden his horse too close, striking me and spoiling a wolf catch. This came near causing serious injury. When I saw this stranger ride up, therefore, I decided that I did not want any other riders in the chase. So I rode around, speaking to this stranger, asking him to have a cigarette. I took a cigarette from a package as I offered one to him.

"No, sir, I do not use the weed, I thank you," he said.

We talked a few minutes and there was something about him that appealed to me. He did not swear nor use any slang. I said:

"Well, my friend, we are out here to make a moving picture, to be shown in the White House; I got run over yesterday and I am going to ask you to vacate."

"Very well, Mr. Abernathy," he said. "I do not want to intrude in any way"—and he started to depart.

"Wait just a minute," I said, as I discovered something about his voice and manner that appealed to me. "I want you to stay, for I like you."

About this time, I looked down toward Medicine Creek and saw a monster wolf going right toward one of the moving-picture cameras. A word to my dogs, and we were off. In less than a minute and a half we were within four feet of the wolf. I hit the water in Medicine Creek and all four of the dogs piled into the stream at the same time that the wolf made a dive. Sam Bass, my horse, hit the water at high speed and fell. I was thrown right over against the wolf and dogs, in water above my waist. I made my right-hand stroke, placing my hand in the wolf's mouth.

This was a most powerful wolf. It clamped my hand, pinching me till I was sick. At the same time it clawed me with its front feet, tearing the shirt from my body, only the collar being left, with a handkerchief which I had tied around my neck.

The wolf was pulling into mid-stream all of the time as we struggled. Its claws were tearing my clothes. I was pulled under the water and by this time was in water ten feet deep. The wolf ducked me and then I would duck the wolf. I guess we ducked each other a half dozen times. The wolf had a death-like grip on my right hand and never did release it. Had I been able to get loose I believe I would have swam out, for I was nearly exhausted.

I was just about ready to give up all hope of getting out alive, when I felt a strong hand take hold of the handkerchief around my neck, and pull me slowly toward the bank into shallower water. I looked up to see who it was, and I saw that it was the man with the sorrel horse!

When this stranger turned me loose in that mud and water, I had one more scuffle with the wolf. Sim Shepherd, who swam his horse across the creek above where I was, came to my aid. The two of us carried the wolf up the bank. It weighed 127 pounds.

Most of this picture was caught by the movie camera. It was a thriller. After I had wired the wolf's muzzle and had it ready for the cage I said,

"Where is the fellow on the sorrel horse who saved my life?"

"I don't know," replied Sim Shepherd. "He has disappeared."

Shepherd called at the top of his voice for the man on the sorrel horse, but nobody answered. Then he called to the boys across the creek, asking them where the man went. They said they did not know.

I feel quite sure that the man on the sorrel horse saved me. He left the place as mysteriously as he came. If it hadn't been for him, I would not be here to tell the story.

The moving pictures were finished, and I took them to the White House.

"That is the best show that ever has been in the White House," said the President.

CHAPTER XXII

CATCHING WOLVES FOR THE MOVIES

I now tried to resign the marshalship of Oklahoma, but my resignation was not accepted at this time. I told the Department of Justice that I wished to stage a wolf-catching expedition for a nationally known moving-picture firm. The Department gave me a leave of absence.

I went to Oradell, New Jersey, where the picture firm had made arrangements with the Lozier estate, about twenty miles from New York, to stage the exhibition. Sam Bass and two other horses were shipped in a car from Frederick, Oklahoma. Nine trained wolf dogs were in the car. All were brought especially for the movies.

The salary paid was seventeen hundred dollars a day to myself and my two boys.

I was to furnish the twelve wolves. Most of the loafers I borrowed from a Zoo in New York City. I had had experience with five species of wolves, but these were different. Most of them were Canadian lobo, which are a little different from the Rocky Mountain lobo.

I caught the wolves for the movies after they were turned loose in the open. The next morning after the pictures had been completed successfully, I was awakened by an announcement that seven of the wolves had escaped!

These wolves had been lent to me by Director W. T. Hornaday, of the Bronx Park Zoological Gardens, upon the assurance of Colonel Theodore Roosevelt that I was dependable and reliable, and that the animals would be safely returned after the pictures were made. These seven wolves had all been enclosed in one large cage. Mr. Lozier, the proprietor of the estate where the pictures had been made, informed me that during the night he had heard a noise that sounded as if the wolves were fighting; and that when he awoke in the morning the cage was empty.

Hastily I called my two boys. Louie ran to the telephone to call for our horses, as I was hurriedly dressing. When Temple looked out and saw the snow, he exclaimed:

"Daddy, we will be polar bears if we get out in this snow!"

Louie called my attention to the fact that, in my haste, I was trying to draw one of his number 3 boots on one of my number 6 feet!

Of course, we raced out to the task of recapturing the fugitive wolves without a bite of breakfast or even a cup of coffee—which did not make the work any easier.

There had been a fall of five or six inches of snow during the night, and the tracks of the wolves were very plain. With my two young sons, I rode from the hotel immediately to the Lozier place.

The wolves were easily tracked in the new-fallen snow. Two of them were found within one hundred yards of the cage from which they had escaped. They did not seem wild or disposed to flee at the sight of men with horses and dogs. On the contrary, they seemed half tame and inclined to be playful in the snow.

With the aid of the dogs, I had little difficulty in recapturing most of the wolves, all being caught on the estate or "ranch" with the exception of one, which succeeded in finding a hole under the high fence as I was pursuing it on Sam Bass. This fence was higher than my head as I sat in the saddle and, of course, entirely too high for the horse to jump. I therefore rode up beside the fence, stood in the saddle and climbed over.

The dogs had followed the wolf through the hole under the fence, and I could hear them fighting it in the brush on the hillside below.

Following the sound of this combat and the tracks in the snow, I soon came in sight of the animals. The wolf started to run, and I followed as fast as I could. My little blue bitch pursued the fugitive, and interfered with its getaway. There was an old rail fence just ahead across an old field. I feared that, if the wolf could get through that, it would be gone beyond recovery. Fortunately, the dog stopped it again and again. Finally, the wolf slashed the dog.

Just as the wolf was approaching the old rail fence, I succeeded in overtaking it. As I struck it on the hips, it whirled to attack me. I gave it my hand and then I went down in the snow, wrestling and rolling with the infuriated animal. In this struggle, the wolf and I rolled into a wash under the fence where the snow had drifted somewhat deeper.

Finally, the animal ceased to struggle so violently, but I was exhausted from the chase that I had made afoot after having to abandon my horse. My lungs seemed afire and ready to burst. I realized that I was powerless to make further exertion other than to maintain my hold on the wolf's lower jaw. Over-heated as I was, lying there in the snow, I realized that I was in a dangerous situation, and that help might not come in hours.

As I lay in the snow under the fence, there passed through my mind the recollection of other incidents in my wolf-hunting experiences in Texas, Oklahoma, Colorado, and New Mexico. I remembered the catching of the first wolf and of the timely arrival of my brother; I thought of the time that Sam Bass fell with me and of how I had to hold him until my dog, Catch, came and looked at me and then raced away for relief; I recalled the charge of the "jingle-bob" steers which surrounded me in a maddened, bawl-ing, pawing mass as I lay on the ground holding a vicious wolf, awaiting the arrival of help; again, I was in the deep water with the big lobo that wanted to drown me, and the rider of the sorrel horse came to my rescue—all of these incidents, and a score of others, passed through my mind like a panorama.

Yet here I was, within twenty-five miles of the greatest city in the world, with its teeming millions of fellow men, and not one who knew of my plight or who would come to my aid.

And then, far up the hillside, I heard the distant voice of my young son, Louie, shouting:

"Are you hurt, Papa?"

I gave an answering hail, and he came to me. He had no wire with which the wolf might be secured or rendered harmless; hence he had to walk back for help, while I had to remain there in the snow with the restless wolf for another half-hour.

Altogether, this was one of the most trying and

anxious experiences that I was ever called upon to undergo in the whole of my life.

If the moving-picture camera could have only got the scenes of these last wolf catches, during the course of that snowy morning, what a wonderful show it would have made!

After resigning the marshalship, I was appointed on the U. S. Secret Service, being assigned to the District of New York City. My first assignment was in Chinatown and the subways. I was required to visit the underworld resorts, among them being the opium dens often frequented by rich and fashionably attired society folks. In company with a U. S. Marshal, one night I "hit the pipe" just to experience the sensation; also to get information from the addicts in the resort.

CHAPTER XXIII

THE ABERNATHY KIDS

During the month of June, about a year after the making of the pictures for the President, my boys Louie and Temple, ages nine and five respectively, asked me for a scuffle. I knew immediately that the youngsters were going to pop some kind of a proposition to me.

Temple, the younger, did most of the talking. (Temple was humored just a little more by me—if there was any humoring—because he was still somewhat of a baby.)

"Daddy, you were raised in West Texas and Mexico, wasn't you?" began Temple, "and you used to ride pitching horses and catch wolves, didn't you?"

"Yes, what about it, Temple?"

"Daddy, we just wanted to ask you, when school is out, to let us get on our horses, and make a little ride from Guthrie to Santa Fe, New Mexico, and back. We will go right across the grounds that you worked over; we have it all mapped out."

They produced a crude map, showing the route, via Estellene, Quitequay, Turkey, and Silverton, on the South Plains of Texas. Louie stepped up and said,

"Papa, I believe we can make the ride all right and we certainly would enjoy it."

I never had refused these boys anything they asked for, and they in turn never had disobeyed me in any way. They were physically and mentally in advance of their age. In reply to them I said,

"Give me till tomorrow to think it over."

I intended spending my vacation on the ranch near Cross Roads, which was one hundred and seventy-five miles on the route to New Mexico. I thought they would have enough riding by the time we reached the ranch; so I decided to tell them that they could go on the trip.

When I returned home the following evening, both boys were anxiously waiting to hear my decision. They were just as playful as ever, with smiles upon their faces. But I could see the inquiring, anxious look in their eyes.

"Well, boys," I said, "I have decided to let you go."

"Great!" said Louie, as he threw his arms around me.

"We have the best Daddy in the world; he never refuses us anything; have you ever thought of that, Bud?" asked Temple.

I decided to give the boys a check book each, placing one hundred dollars in a bank in each account. (I also left instructions with the banker to honor any over-draft.) During the trip, as it turned out, the boys each drew money by check, but usually not more than ten dollars. At nearly every place along the route, the person cashing the check refused to send it for clearance. Instead, the check signed by either of the Abernathy Kids was kept as a souvenir.

Two days after school closed in Guthrie, the boys were in their saddles, headed for the ranch near Cross Roads. I did not go for a week and then went by train to join them.

"Well, Daddy, we want to start for Santa Fe just

as quick as you will let us," said Temple, after telling me how much fun they were having on the ranch.

"Well, boys, I want to make you a proposition: let's stay here awhile and have fun riding and swimming," I said. "You never have seen me ride a wild horse, have you?"

"Yes, Daddy, I have," replied Louie. "Don't you remember when they brought wild horses here, when I was five years old?"

"Now, boys, we will go up here near Cache, and I will buy the meanest horse the Indians have, put my saddle on him, and ride to a finish. I will ride the same horse back home, if you will give up your ride to Santa Fe," I said.

Temple chuckled and said: "Gee! that would be great, Daddy, but you can do that when we come back home; we have been reading about Santa Fe, New Mexico, up in the mountains, and we are anxious to see it."

Louie said,

"Daddy, you told us we could go. Now do what you said you would."

"All right, boys," I said, still thinking that they would want to come back home when they got a taste of gyp water out near Estellene, Texas.

Two days later, the boys started from the ranch on their ride to Santa Fe. I returned to Guthrie, feeling blue and lonesome. However, letters received with pictures of the boys came from mayors of different towns along the route. I knew that the boys were safe and were being well cared for.

Fourteen days following their departure, a telegram came from Governor George Currie, of New Mexico, saying,

"The Kids are here and are as fat as pigs; come out."

Governor Currie was a former Rough Rider who served in Cuba with Roosevelt. He was my personal friend. I boarded the next train for Santa Fe and, upon arrival at the Governor's mansion, I met the boys. Temple apparently had taken charge of the mansion, as he was giving orders to the Portuguese servants, who seemed quite ready to take them.

"Come with us to the piano, Dad; we want to sing you a new song we have learned," said Temple. They played and sang the song, entitled: "No, Not One." When the boys reached the part which says, "Jesus knows all about our struggles," Temple would say, "schuggles," for he couldn't pronounce the word "struggles."

"Did you have any struggles coming out here?" I asked.

Temple replied, saying that they had gone without food for a whole day while in the mountains of New Mexico. "You bet, Papa, I never left a town but what I had everything tied on my saddle after that."

"Tell him about the jackass getting after you," said Louie to Temple.

"Yes, Papa, a jackass ran me about six miles, but I threw the spurs into old Geronimo and outran him. Bud was galloping along ahead, laughing at me." (Louie was riding Sam Bass. Temple added that Louie didn't get far ahead.)

I received a letter in Guthrie with a fictitious name and initials signed to it. The letter was writ-

ten on a brown sugar sack. Instead of a pen or
pencil, a lead bullet was used. Only the envelope
bore the address of the Marshal. The letter was
as follows:

"I don't like a hair on your head, but I do like
the stuff that is in these kids. We shadowed them
through the worst part of New Mexico, to see that
they were not harmed by sheep herders or other mean
men. A. Z. Y."

I took this letter to Al Jennings, ex-outlaw, and
asked,

"Al, what friend of yours wrote this?" Al, after
looking it over, replied,

"That is old Arizona, the fellow who wanted to
kill you the time you asked him to give up, in the
Haystack Mountains, in Western Oklahoma." I
recalled the incident, where two of Arizona's party
were killed and he got away from us.

This goes to show that there is something good in
all men, even though they are outlaws. This des-
perado would have killed me at the drop of a hat,
yet he was honorable enough to protect my innocent
boys. I appreciated the spirit of that letter, even if
it was written with a bullet.

I tried to persuade the boys to accompany me
home on the train, but they would not listen to
this. "We have been over one route and we want to
go back another, through Mangum, Hobart, and
Chickasha," said Louie.

Governor Currie suggested that the boys carry some
kind of a gun while traveling through the sheep
country in New Mexico. He feared the herders
might rob them, either of their money or horses. I
purchased a single-barrel shotgun and a box of car-

tridges loaded with buckshot. I also instructed Louie
to use the gun if anybody molested them.

"If a man tries to bother you, just take the drop
on him," I said.

"But what if this man does not stop when I point
the gun at him?" asked Louie.

"Defend yourself by pulling the trigger," I replied.

I rode with the boys from Santa Fe to Las Vegas,
over the mountain pass. I sent the horse back by a
revenue officer. It took two days to make the trip
over the rough climb. I boarded the train at Las
Vegas for Guthrie, leaving the boys to make the ride
home by themselves.

Upon reaching Oklahoma City the boys were met
by a brass band and a large delegation of citizens.
The crowd held the boys for half an hour. About
fifty women gathered around Temple, the smaller
of the two, asking him questions about dangers of
the long journey. One woman exclaimed,

"Why did your mother let you go?"

"My mother is dead," was Temple's reply. At
this, the woman grabbed the boy and started to
scream,

"Where is your father. I want to tell him how
crazy he is, to let small boys like you go on such a
trip."

"There's my Papa," replied Temple, pointing his
finger toward me as I stood a few feet away.

Upon reaching the city's edge, the band and pro-
cession met the boys as they were coming from El
Reno, escorting them to the Lee-Huckins Hotel.
Later they rode to Guthrie that day.

Louie told me, upon reaching Oklahoma City,
of the only illness during the trip. In instructing

Louie to look out for the younger child, I had given him a bottle of castor oil, thinking Temple might need it.   While passing through the inland town of Turkey, near the edge of the cap rock, on the South Plains of Texas, Temple became sick, so castor oil was offered for a remedy.   The boy thought this was good for almost any illness.   But Temple needed anything but this for a remedy.   He had been drinking gyp water, which alone was sufficient to supply the needed remedy.   "Of all the medicine in the world, I don't need castor oil; this gyp water is ruining me," cried Temple in protest.

Both Temple and Louie, while on their long ride to and from Sante Fe, carried a little Testament. They were instructed to pray each night before going to sleep.   Both of the boys promised me that they would pray each night.   And, upon their return, they told me they kept their promise.

I had made all arrangements to go along with Theodore Roosevelt on his big game hunt in South Africa, when forced to cancel the trip because of the sudden death of Mrs. Abernathy.   I did this because I could not leave my six children, the youngest of whom was only a baby, a month old.

A few months later, Roosevelt was on his way home from the famous hunt.   His friends and admirers, by the thousands, were flocking to New York, to give the ex-President a warm greeting.   Naturally, I was among them.   The Kids heard me talking about making the trip; so they begged to go along.

"We have seen the rough side of life; let us ride our horses to New York, Daddy, and see the good part of the country," begged Louie.

I decided to let the Kids go to Gotham. They rode from the Abernathy ranch at Cross Roads, arriving in the Osage Nation, where Geronimo, Temple's horse, played out. Temple then bought a pinto pony, paying eighty-five dollars for the animal.

Eight days after the Kids left the Abernathy ranch, I received the first news from them: a letter came from Louie, at St. Joseph, Mo. Louie told about buying the pony for Temple, also about a horse race the Kids had.

"Temple got the idea that the pinto pony could outrun Sam Bass, and I matched him for a race," wrote Louie. "We ran about a quarter-mile, when Sam went wild, running over a stump. Sam hurt my leg, but I am all right now."

I had been very uneasy over the safety of the Kids, despite the fact that I was busily engaged in Court at Oklahoma City. An important murder trial was on in the Federal Court at the time. After the Kids left St. Joseph, Mo., where they met Tom Walker, one of my former deputies, they went on east. Deputy Wiley Haynes, in the Osage Nation, had met the boys at Hominy, at the time they bought the horse. They had named the pinto after Haynes.

By reading the newspapers, I had no trouble in keeping tab on the Kids as they journeyed east. The farther east they went, the more attention they attracted. In every city and hamlet along the route, they were a sensation. They were royally entertained at every stop. They were shown every sight in the big cities of the East, which was a wonderful education for them.

William H. Taft, then President, greeted them in

the White House at Washington.   Joe Cannon, then
speaker, took the Kids before the session of Congress,
introducing them to all the members.   He then took
them to the Senate, where they were also introduced.
They remained in Washington for a week before re-
suming the journey toward New York.

Independence Square, Philadelphia, and the Betsy
Ross home, where the first American flag was de-
signed, were shown to the boys.   At Independence
Square, they saw the Liberty Bell, also the first
capitol building, where President George Washington was inaugurated the second time.   Upon leaving Philadelphia, they rode to Trenton, New Jersey,
where I met them.

Woodrow Wilson, Governor of New Jersey at that
time, sent an invitation to the Kids, asking them to
visit the executive offices at the New Jersey capital.
They had planned to accept the invitation, but their
time was short, so they hurried on to New York.

Riding on to New York, the Kids were met at the
Bowery and escorted to the Breslin Hotel, by a squad
of one hundred bluecoats, thirty of the squad being
mounted on horses.   Thousands of curious ones
thronged into the streets, hoping to meet the Kids.

Two of the biggest of the police carried the Kids
upon their shoulders through the crowd.   One woman
became hysterical and, after reaching Temple,
pulled his hair—she wanted a lock of it for a souvenir,
it appeared.

With the Kids I remained at the Breslin Hotel
for a month.   In order to get away from the hotel
without being stampeded, it became necessary for
the Kids to be separated.   Doctor Wainwright,
physician at the hotel, took Temple, and I took

Louie, when the Kids were being shown about New York City.

Entering one of the theatres on Broadway where Eva Tanguay was giving a star performance, the Kids were placed in a seat close to the front. Miss Tanguay tried to pull Temple to the stage, but was stopped by Doctor Wainwright. Then she tossed a beautiful bouquet of flowers into his lap. A quartette of the troupe composed a song in honor of the Kids, which they sang. The song had the following words:

> "Pony boys, tony boys,
> Oh, you Oklahoma boys;
> Now you're here,
> Give us a cheer!"

Upon finishing the last line of the song, the entire crowd cheered in honor of the Abernathy Kids.

A wireless message signed by them was sent to Theodore Roosevelt, at sea, inquiring as to the arrival date of the ex-President, for they wanted to meet "Teddy" at sea. In company with me, the Kids boarded a revenue cutter and were taken to meet Colonel Roosevelt.

As we climbed aboard the ship, Roosevelt grasped my hand and exclaimed,

"Marshal, I read about you while in the jungles of Africa—about the Harrah bank robbery. How I wish you had gone with me! But I know what you did you had to do: it was your duty."

Colonel Roosevelt then shook hands with the Kids, saying,

"God bless you, my boys! you have made a strenuous ride to meet me."

A fleet of revenue cutters escorted the ex-President's ship from quarantine station into the harbor. The reception was most impressive. The salute given the ex-President, by guns from the many ships, in coming ashore, was almost continuous. I never will forget that great demonstration.

When we reached the dock, a large number of Rough Riders were waiting to greet their former leader in war. Sam Bass and Wiley Haynes, the horses ridden by the Abernathy Kids, were placed at the head of the mounted column in the parade. The line of march was up Fifth Avenue.

Thirty days later the Brush Automobile Co. presented the Kids with a one-cylinder roadster. We shipped the horses back by rail, and the Kids returned to Oklahoma in the car, riding by themselves. They were photographed in nearly every city along the route, their pictures appearing in nearly every large newspaper from New York to Oklahoma City.

Several months after the motor-car trip to Oklahoma, the Brush Auto firm requested the Kids to come to New York City to attend the Automobile Show. The Kids made the trip. At that event Thompson and Dundee, famous New York showmen, offered them a prize of ten thousand dollars on condition that they ride from the Atlantic to the Pacific within sixty days. With my consent, the Kids accepted.

Before the Coast-to-Coast trip, Thompson and Dundee engaged the Kids to stage a "Donkey and Elephant Race" from New York City to Washington.

This was a burlesque on the two political parties. Temple rode the donkey and Louie the elephant.

The Kids had more fun out of this race than any other staged during their career as riders. Louie says he got the most fun out of watching the horses (there were still horses on the road in those days) become frightened and run away. (Nearly all horses are afraid of elephants.)

At Philadelphia the race was stopped on account of the sore feet of the elephant. The Humane Society took a hand in the affair, and threatened to bring court action to prevent alleged brutality to animals. The elephant had been placed in a corral, where veterinarians were called. I learned of the trouble and went to Philadelphia, hoping to settle the argument.

When I tangled up with that officer there was no sign of "brotherly love" shown. He ran to me and asked,

"Is your name Abernathy?"

I replied, "I haven't changed it."

"Well, I am going to have to arrest you," continued the officer. I laughed at this threat.

"Are you laughing at me? This is a very serious charge!" he continued, shouting. He placed his hand on my arm, asking me to "go along."

"Turn me loose!" I answered, knocking the hand off my shoulder.

But we had to call off the race. The elephant really had sore feet.

Meanwhile, plans for the Kids to make the ride from the Atlantic to the Pacific were being made. A week before their departure, however, the Kids rode to Oyster Bay, for a visit at the home of Theodore Roosevelt.

Every morning during the Oyster Bay visit, the Kids went riding with the ex-President. On the morning the boys were to leave the Roosevelt home, I took a moving-picture camera-man along to get photos of Colonel Roosevelt and the Kids. Just before they left, Colonel Roosevelt called them into a private room, saying,

"I want to talk to you for a minute."

I noticed that the door of the room adjoining the reception room was ajar. I was sitting near two reporters and the camera-man, and I overheard part of the ex-President's talk.

"Boys, I want you to remember that I think as much of you two as your own father does, if that is possible," said the Colonel. "I have noticed your pictures in New York papers nearly every day for thirty days, and I realize what a fuss is being made over you. I cannot see that all of this fuss has turned your heads, or spoiled you in the least. That is why I am so proud of you. Now, if any one says anything good about you, just resolve that they will never regret it, and that you will do something else to cause them to say better things of you. If they say anything bad about you, pay no attention to it, unless they carry it too far."

Colonel Roosevelt talked to the Kids for a considerable length of time, giving them sound, fatherly advice and wishing them well on their long journey. He kissed both of them as they left.

A minute after twelve o'clock midnight that night, the Kids rode their horses into the Atlantic Ocean, at Coney Island, and started on their long horseback ride. More than ten thousand persons gathered to see them make the start.

All parks in the city were closed at twelve o'clock. The Kids rode out of Luna Park just at closing time. Under the offer, if the Kids were to win the ten thousand dollars, they had to ride into the Pacific, through Golden Gate Park, San Francisco, within sixty days.

Louie was riding Sam Bass, the famous wolf horse, and Temple, Wiley Haynes. The distance to be covered was a total of 3,619 miles. The contract provided that the boys were not to eat or sleep under a roof during the journey.

They sent telegrams nearly every night to Thompson and Dundee, giving details as to mileage covered and success of the trip. Upon reaching the desert in the Western States, however, they found it impossible to send wires every night.

The route passed through the cities of Buffalo, Chicago, Omaha, Cheyenne, Reno, Sacramento, and San Francisco.

In their journey the Kids often rode alongside the railroad tracks, and railroad crews would offer to load the horses and carry them through the desert. This the Kids refused to permit. They remembered the good advice given to them by the ex-President. They decided it was better to lose honestly, if they must lose, than to win ten thousand dollars dishonestly.

The only unhappy event of the trip was the death of Sam Bass. This faithful friend foundered and died suddenly near Cheyenne, Wyoming.

Louie and Temple rode their horses into the Pacific Ocean at last—but only after sixty-two days. They had lost the prize! But they had not cheated.

At the end of the trip, the Kids received an offer from a vaudeville circuit of three hundred dollars a week. The engagement would have taken them over the entire nation and Canada, but I objected. The Kids appeared a total of about six weeks before I took them off the stage at Denver. They returned thence to the ranch in Oklahoma.

I placed them in a military school at San Antonio, Texas, and I then went on to Mexico, where I was then employed by the Madero Government, in secret-service work.

Two years after the Ocean-to-Ocean ride, the Kids rode a motorcycle from the Abernathy Ranch to New York City. Both rode on the same cycle, which had two seats. They met their sister, Kittie Joe, who had finished school. The Kids shipped the motorcycle home, making the return trip on the train.

CHAPTER XXIV

"CATCH" THE DOG HERO

Writers since the beginning of time have sounded the praises of dogs. My life story would not be complete without honorable mention of Catch, a Scotch-shepherd male, who became mine during the early days of Old Greer County, Oklahoma, and to whom I owe my life.

Catch was a mere puppy when he was given to my father. We were living on the ranch near Cross Roads. There was no bridge over North Fork of Red River at Robert's Crossing. The river was high and a stranger who was trying to cross got mired with his team and wagon. The quicksand was about to take the outfit under when the stranger swam the river, seeking aid from my father. Quickly my father took his team and pulled the outfit to dry land. As a reward the stranger gave him the puppy.

Catch soon exhibited signs of a remarkable ability to guard small children in the Abernathy home. It was decided therefore to keep him as a pet, and for the protection of the youngsters. He proved to be afraid of nothing. He never fought without cause, but never lost a fight.

I had never intended to let Catch go along when I caught wolves. The way he came to go along the first time was as follows. I once established a camp for a wolf chase on Deep Red Creek. After being there for several days, I went home to the ranch for the week-end. Upon going back to the camp I took Catch along.

Doctor W. W. Cox, of Frederick, and my half-brother Felix Thompson, rode up to the camp about noon on the third day of the chase. They told me of their desire to see me catch a wolf that day.

I was ready to go, so we three rode south toward Red River. I left Catch tied up at camp, but somehow he got loose. Before getting more than one hundred yards out of the camp I noticed Catch following. I scolded him, then rode after him, chasing him under the wagon. I started out once more, but, after riding a mile and a half across the prairie, I observed that he was following again about two hundred yards behind. I stopped this time and called Catch to me and whipped him—though not very hard, because I thought so much of him. Then I chased him back to the camp again.

After we traveled about a mile from where I whipped Catch, we jumped a big wolf. This wolf was a running fiend. (Wolves are like horses—some can easily outrun others.) From appearances, it seemed almost impossible to overtake it. The dogs and horses were doing their best. Sam Bass, my horse, was in the lead, but it was all he could do to keep up with this wolf. He took me to within about twenty feet of the wolf, when suddenly the animal disappeared over the bank. Sam Bass was going so fast it was impossible to stop. He plunged over the bank, his front feet hitting a sort of a bench about ten feet below.

Hitting as he did, this drop seemed to turn Sam Bass sidewise, causing him to fall on me. My right foot was caught in the stirrup, and I realized that unless I held Sam Bass down by the horn of the saddle I should be dragged to death. Sam Bass tried several times to free himself by getting up, but I clung to the horn of the saddle, making it impossible for him to get on his feet. My right ankle was holding the bulk of his weight. This was paining me dreadfully, but there was nothing else for me to do but hold the horse down.

In the race, Sam Bass had run so far ahead of Doctor Cox and Felix, my half-brother, that they had lost sight of us and returned to the camp. They were not used to riding so fast.

I held Sam Bass for what seemed like hours, but which was probably not more than fifteen minutes. I could not get to the knife in the right pocket of my trousers, to cut the stirrup leather: Sam Bass was lying upon that leg.

I wondered, as I lay there, what would happen to me, when suddenly I saw the woolly head of Catch at the top of the bank over which Sam Bass had fallen with me. The dog whined and howled for a minute, then disappeared. Something seemed to tell me that he would bring aid.

I learned afterward that Catch returned to the camp, running up to my half-brother, and began howling, then ran off a short distance toward where Sam Bass and myself were lying. The dog continued to howl, bark, and run in this fashion.

Doctor Cox, who noticed how excited the dog was, said:

"Felix, we had better follow that dog; there is something wrong." Felix replied,

"Yes, Jack has had trouble."

Catch would run ahead, they told me afterward, then jump back toward the riders, as they were coming to my rescue. Finally I heard the beat of horses' hoofs, and the barking of Catch. The dog led Doctor Cox and Felix to the edge of the bluff, just over where I was holding Sam Bass.

"Are you dead?" asked Doctor Cox, as he looked at us.

"How could a dead man hold a horse down?" I replied. "Uncinch the saddle, so Sam Bass can get up, but hold him as you do, for this horse will run as soon as he gets up."

Felix uncinched the girth and Sam Bass bounced up instantly. He resaddled Sam Bass, and we all started for the camp. Upon quick examination, Doctor Cox discovered that one bone in my ankle was out of place. He said this ankle must be placed in a plaster cast.

"Will this interfere with my wolf catching?" I asked.

"Not if you catch them on one leg," the Doctor replied.

I rode with Doctor Cox to Frederick, fourteen miles away, where the cast was placed. I then rode back to the camp. My ankle pained me nearly all night, but it seemed to "get easy" about daylight. I went on catching wolves, using my left leg in landing. I did not have to run after the wolves. But ever since that day my foot has pained me, and I cannot stand upon it for any length of time.

After that day I never whipped Catch again.

Catch had earned the right to go on wolf hunts with me, and became one of my regular companions on these adventures. Of the many stories of his loyalty and his fighting qualities on these hunts, I shall tell just one—in which he saved my life once more.

One day I drove out to Deep Red Creek, twenty miles from any house. Then I stopped under some large trees near the bank of the creek, throwing my brake, and tying the lines. Then I grabbed my rifle and shot three squirrels from the very tree that I was camped under. I then took out my team, unsaddled my horse, and chained the dogs to the trees. After building a fire I started to prepare my supper, which consisted of squirrel stew, black coffee, and cold biscuits. That meal hit the spot.

After eating and doing the chores—feeding my horses and seeing that the dogs were properly cared for—I crawled into my wagon. The evening being beautiful, I hated to go to bed so early, but knowing the strenuous job I had for the next day, off I went to sleep.

About eleven o'clock I was awakened by Sam Bass, whom I had tied to the front wheel of my wagon in order to keep him safe from outlaws. (Many of them wanted him badly, for he was the fastest horse I had ever been on.) Sam was lunging against the rope, snorting; and I realized that he saw something out of the ordinary. I got up in a jiffy, picking up my six-shooter; and, dropping to my knees in front of the wagon, tried to "sky-light" around the camp. I noticed Sam looking straight east across the creek. To my surprise, I heard wolves snapping and growling, which was music to my soul. I patted Sam, got back in the wagon, and went to sleep again.

I could not have been asleep more than an hour and a half when I was awakened by human voices, as I thought. I seized my gun a second time; and, as I got out of the front of the wagon, the voices became louder. This time I found that it was owls in the trees above talking to each other. That too made my heart beat with joy, for I had always heard that owls talking to each other was a sign of good luck.

Once again I crawled back into the wagon, sleeping through till five o'clock; when I was awakened by the rain that was spattering against the canvas coverings. The beauty of the night before had vanished. Much as I dislike getting out into the cold rain, I realized that in this kind of weather the wolves would be prowling. I felt sure that I would get a loafer. I dressed hurriedly, prepared my coffee, saddled Sam Bass, and unsnapped two of my little greyhounds. Then I crossed the creek and was on my way, peering in every direction for a wolf.

Besides the four greyhounds left tied to the tree I had chained Catch to the wagon.

I had ridden about four hundred yards when I came to a small stream. Here I noticed my greyhounds whining, staying close to my horse's heels, and looking straight ahead.

I could not see anything because of the trees and brush along the bank of the stream, so I rolled off my horse, and stooped down. Looking directly across the stream—not over a hundred yards away—I saw two large loafer wolves. Evidently they had not sighted the dogs, so I leaped into the saddle again, spoke to the dogs, and started to cross the stream. I did not know how deep it was, and didn't care; for it had been about a month since I had caught a lobo wolf, and I knew that to get one meant fifty dollars for me.

My horse plunged into the water, which was about ten to fifteen feet deep. The splash attracted the lobos' attention, but they had not yet sighted the dogs. When I reached solid ground my two little dogs were right by me. Seeing the dogs, the wolves broke, and the race was on.

A steep hill, very difficult for my horse to climb, impeded my progress, and my dogs were now within twenty feet of the wolves. After we reached the top of the hill the wolves made a turn to the right, heading south and down this hill, so the dogs did not gain much.

Upon reaching the flat in the valley the dogs and the wolves turned back west toward the camp. They had separated, and I no longer could see Abe, the old greyhound; but the big wolf, which Blue Bitch was after, was running almost neck and neck with the dog. I was begging Blue Bitch to take hold. Soon they leaped off a little bank where the ground was about two feet lower nearly all around for about an acre. As I went over this bank I did not observe whether the wolf nipped the dog, or the dog the wolf; but I know that I hit the ground and, having on my slicker, I felt a bit awkward.

The wolf at once leaped at my throat. His mouth was within three inches of my stomach when I caught him. We wrestled, we scuffled, and finally went down together, with the wolf desperately trying to free himself. I was on top, but wondering what I would do, since the horse had gone with the wire that I needed to wire the mouth of the wolf.

Just then I noticed the second wolf crouched in a cat-like position, ready to spring upon me. I could see blood on his mouth and nose, and thought he had killed Abe. Meanwhile, I could hear Catch at the wagon barking for dear life. I knew that the wolf would make his spring very quickly and, unless aid came at once, I was doomed.

Suddenly there was a rush at my left and I saw a dark object dart off the bank and attack the wolf.

"It's Catch! It's Catch!" The dog had broken his chain and come to join in the fight. "Get him, Catch! Get him, Catch!" I shouted. "Take a throat hold—get up again, Old Timer—the chain on your throat is helping you! You can't help but win! Fight over this way, where I can get a kick at him!"

I kicked once, allowing myself to get off the wolf's body on which I was lying, but the kick failed to reach.

"Work for his throat, Catch! Work for his throat! Never mind his feet! You're gaining! Oh, my God, he's got him by the throat. Hold on, Catch! Go deeper! Crush him! You've got him, Catch, if you don't turn loose."

I kept shouting while the dogs worked. Catch, with a gameness I have never seen excelled by a dog, kept this hold; and, aided by the heroic Abe, soon had the wolf on the ground dead.

However, I was not yet out of danger, for I was still struggling to conquer my own wolf. Presently I heard a shout:

"Hello, Jack! What in the h - - - are you doing there? Gad! You've hubbed a big one this time. That's the scoundrel that's been killing our cattle."

Looking up, I saw Cal, a line rider for Waggoner.

"Shut up, Cal, and bring me some wire right quick or I'll be cut down! This wolf's chewing on me right now," I said.

"I have nothing but some barbed wire about two feet long that I was aiming to splice a fence with."

"Well, unwrap it right quick and get the barbs out and give it to me!"

"I'd leave the barbs in it," suggested Cal.

"No! No! I want to save this wolf. I'm the only one that's hurt."

Cal gave me the wire and in a few minutes I had Mr. Wolf where he could do no more harm.

Catch continued to act as protector of my children for years. After I moved my family to Guthrie, Catch still followed the children to school. The street-car conductors were of course forbidden to permit dogs to ride upon the cars. One conductor had most of his clothes torn off when he attempted to put Catch off. After that the conductors let the dog ride. Everybody in Guthrie approved, for they knew about the faithfulness of this heroic dog.

Among the famous fights in which Catch took part was one with a white bulldog in Guthrie. This bulldog was the champion fighter of the State of Kansas. The owner of the bulldog came to my home to see the dogs, especially Catch. When the bulldog came into our house it growled at one of the children. Instantly Catch leaped for it, and the fight was on. Women and men for a block around watched the contest and the attempt to separate the dogs. The owner of the bulldog was badly bitten while trying to pull the animals apart. Finally an iron clamp had to be used to break the bulldog's hold on Catch.

Catch lived to be about fourteen years old. Then a mad dog bit him, and I had to kill my old friend. I never hated to do anything so badly in my life.

CHAPTER XXV

WOLF BITES ARE DANGEROUS

The mention of rabies in the last chapter reminds me that a great many people who have listened to my stories of wolf catching want to know why I haven't died from rabies or blood poisoning from wolf bites. A word about this will not be out of place after a chapter about Catch, who lost *his* life because of man's great fear of the dread disease of rabies.

It is well known among doctors that rabies may originate among mad wolves. That none of the many wolves which have bitten me were mad was simply a matter of luck.

As for blood poisoning, I did develop a serious case as the result of one wolf bite on my hand. This bite was an accident. I had made a catch during a chase in the Wichita Mountains. The lobo weighed one hundred and seventeen pounds. After catching the animal, I wired its jaws in the usual manner; then threw it across my saddle. Just as I started to get into the saddle, the wolf broke the wire around its mouth and nose. Instantly it bit me across the left finger, cutting the bone nearly in two. I got hold of the wolf with my right hand, this time wiring the jaws for keeps. Using a bottle of wolf medicine which I carried, I then tied up the wounded finger with gauze. The wound did not stop me. I kept on chasing and catching wolves for five more days. Then my hand began to swell, and the pain was so terrific that I started for Guthrie. Three different doctors were called in after a serious case of blood poisoning developed. My arm turned black to the shoulder.

"I hate to tell you, Abernathy," said Doctor Melvin, "but the only way to give you a fighting chance to live is to take your arm off at the shoulder."

"A one-armed man couldn't fight, Doctor, so just let it stay on me," was my reply.

Four hours later I lapsed into unconsciousness. All I know about what happened was told to me afterwards.

When things looked so bad for me, my chief deputy marshal, Chris Madsen, decided to call Dr. Black, of Tecumseh, an old-time country doctor known all over Oklahoma as an expert in treating blood poisoning. About three o'clock in the morning he called Deputy Johnny Jones at Shawnee, to get him to call Dr. Black. But, by a rare piece of bad luck, Madsen had recently had a fight with the telephone company over some question of service, and had instructed all his deputies neither to send nor receive long-distance calls. Consequently, Jones refused to answer the call—and I almost lost my life.

The next morning Mrs. Jones happened to see in the Shawnee morning paper a paragraph saying that I was dead. Jones forgot all his orders and called up Madsen at once.

"Is the Marshal dead?"

"No! He is very much alive," was the reply. "I called you a few hours ago, and you would not answer the phone. Get old Doctor Black, at

Tecumseh; bring him to Guthrie if you have to handcuff him."

Deputy Johnny Jones went after Doctor Black, driving overland to Guthrie in a two-horse rig. Three doctors and a nurse were in the room when Doctor Black arrived. Black did not speak to any one present, but rushed to me, smelling my breath.

"If I can keep him alive twelve hours, there is a chance for him," said Doctor Black.

Dr. Black remained with me for three days. On the second day after he arrived, I was already able to sit up in bed. He ran out of medicine and made a trip to Oklahoma City to get an additional supply. He would not buy medicine in Guthrie.

Soon after my recovery, I left for California. Upon returning to Oklahoma five years later, I asked about Doctor Black. I was informed that he was ill, but that he had given the secret of his blood-poison treatment to another doctor. The other doctor died, however, and Black himself recovered. Later he died, and took his secret with him to the grave.

CHAPTER XXVI

A MILLION OVERNIGHT

Soon after the World War broke out I resigned my position with the Mexican Government to enter the oil business as a wildcat driller. I located at Wichita Falls, Texas. At this time there had already been considerable oil development in North Texas. Oil fortunes had been made by a large number of operators in the fields around Electra, but there had been no boom. I took up a block of ten thousand acres surrounding the Abernathy ranch in what then was a part of Tillman County. A test well was drilled on the Pickeral Farm, a mile south of the Abernathy homestead. This well proved to be a "duster" at a depth of three thousand feet.

Fortune smiled upon me as a result of the completion of the famous discovery well near the town of Burkburnett, Wichita County, Texas. The gusher was a regular wild, spouting geyser of wealth. Had the oil rained gold dollars as it sprayed its fortune-making fluid over most of the one thousand acres owned by the Fowler interests, there would have been no more excitement than that which existed as result of the great discovery. Excitement was the wildest known in Texas since the days of the historic Spindletop, at Beaumont, in 1900.

During the World War period, high-gravity crude oil was in great demand throughout the world. Burkburnett's discovery well was producing oil that sold for three dollars and a half a barrel. Production from the discovery gusher was claimed to be at the rate of twenty-five thousand barrels every twenty-four hours. Original owners of interests in the Fowler No. 1 well, were paid off at the rate of twenty-five thousand for every dollar invested at the beginning of drilling.

Burkburnett was the first stop out of Wichita Falls on the newly constructed Wichita Falls and Northwestern Railway, through the former Big Pasture to Frederick, Altus, Mangum, Elk City, Woodward and Forgan, Oklahoma. Burkburnett had been just a whistling station. The town had less than one thousand population at the time oil was discovered. Wichita Falls, the county seat, had eight thousand.

Burkburnett's townsite was about three miles south of Red River, and the city of Wichita Falls was about fifteen miles farther south. Burkburnett originally was a part of the vast ranch holdings of Capt. S. Burke Burnett, the multi-millionaire Texas cattle ranchman. It became a city of more than forty thousand inside of thirty days following the completion of the Fowler No. 1 oiler. Within a few months, Wichita Falls jumped to a city estimated at one hundred and fifty thousand.

Every city, town, and county for miles around the Burkburnett area had rapid increase in population as result of the oil discovery. The great boom extended into Tillman County, Oklahoma, the district including most all of the land traveled over by President Roosevelt and his party during the famous wolf hunt staged fourteen years previously.

I was at Burkburnett, within a half mile of the Fowler No. 1, when the giant gusher began to blow mud, water and oil out of the hole. I had been watching the well for several weeks while drilling my own wildcat on the Pickeral farm near the Abernathy homestead in Oklahoma. Fowler No. 1 was located about one hundred yards from the road leading into the town. The well was at the north-east corner of the townsite.

Men with millions of dollars flocked into Burkburnett. Millionaires were being made over night as result of rapid oil development. Being on the ground floor, I accumulated oil leases that potentially were worth millions. At one time I had more than sixty thousand dollars in cash in banks, to say nothing of the valuable oil properties I owned, which were yet to be developed.

It was my fortune to become an independent oil operator. I was one of the first to take advantage of opportunities in the greatest oil boom of that day.

Nearly every lot in the townsite of Burkburnett either had producing wells or was included in a drilling site. The derricks were so close to each other in some parts of the town that persons could walk from one well to the other by stepping from platform to platform. The owner of almost any lot in this town could sell it for from one to five thousand dollars.

Land surrounding Burkburnett townsite sold at five thousand dollars an acre at the beginning of the oil boom. I paid fifteen thousand for three-fourths of an acre located in the North-west Extension, a tract adjoining the original townsite. Two wells, each drilled to a total depth of nineteen hundred feet, were completed as gushers. Because of the lack of pipeline facilities, neither of these gushers was permitted to flow its entire output of oil. From the showing made in these gushers, either of these two producers was estimated to be good for upwards of ten thousand barrels daily, initial flow.

Oil from the two wells which I drilled was sold at three dollars and a half a barrel. After getting back nearly all of the cash spent for drilling, I sold one-half interest in the producing property to Tom Flynn, of the Bradford Supply Co., for which I received sixty-five thousand dollars, the money being all paid in cash on the barrel head. Later, I sold the other one-half interest to Flynn for the same amount. I had been receiving about seven thousand dollars every fifteen days from the sale of crude oil, from one-half interest in the two wells. I operated the property for about three months before selling out to Flynn.

In addition to my oil production, I was making large sums of money selling and buying leases; also in the drilling of wells under contract. I operated three rigs in the field for eight months. I received about fifteen thousand dollars for every hole drilled to a total depth of nineteen hundred feet. Of this money, drillers received from fifteen to eighteen dollars a day each. Two shifts of men were employed on each well, a crew consisting of the driller, tool pusher, and five "rough necks." Each crew worked twelve hours.

My producing oil property was located about one-half mile south and east of the famous Burk-Waggoner gusher drilled by Bob Waggoner and Associates. Bob was a relative of Tom Waggoner, pioneer cattle ranchman, who had taken part in the wolf chase staged for the entertainment of President

Roosevelt. Tom Waggoner, the ranchman, refused eighty millions in cash for a blanket lease on the Waggoner ranch property, during the oil boom. This huge sum, the largest ever offered for such a tract of leases, was from one of the major oil companies.

A number of test wells were drilled just across the river from Burkburnett, but no production was found except a few wells that were drilled in the river bed. Farther over in Cotton County, between Walters and Lawton, there was a big boom as the result of producing wells.

Many of the fortune hunters who visited the Burkburnett oil district carried huge rolls of currency in their pockets. It was nothing unusual to hear of oil operators walking around with "spot cash" ready to close almost any kind of deals.

Hotels were unable to begin to accommodate the people who swarmed into Wichita Falls and Burkburnett during the boom. A single bed for one night, in the cheapest kind of a hotel, was taken quickly at two dollars. All hotels placed two beds in a room. Over at Grandfield, a small town across Red River, a brick hotel with large rooms had from twelve to sixteen beds in each room. Each bed brought two dollars a night. Wichita Falls hotels, after renting all rooms, rented out the chairs in the lobby, at fifty cents a night, for sleeping purposes.

Seeing the demand for houses, I bought a number of rent houses in Wichita Falls. I noticed that many house owners displayed signs, "No children allowed." Having a large family of motherless children of my own, I realized fully what such a sign meant to a family. I thought to myself, "Must a man kill the children to please the landlords?" So I provided a lot of houses, using the sign: "People without children need not apply." As a result, I rented all of my houses quickly to people with children, and I also had a waiting list of applicants from prospective tenants.

I bought a hotel of twenty-four sleeping rooms, a dining room, and kitchen. (I was offered eighty-five thousand dollars for the hotel within five months. It had cost me twenty-two thousand five hundred.) This hotel was in the close-in business district of Wichita Falls.

Fully twenty thousand transient people were on the streets, in the offices, oil-stock exchanges, and depots at Wichita Falls every day of the oil boom. There were thousands of oil workers.

Office space became so scarce in Wichita Falls that huge prices were paid for old store and warehouse rooms to be remodeled into offices. Rooms, upstairs or down, were partitioned off into "stalls," some being not more than twelve feet square. Wooden or iron railings were used to fence off the stalls. After there were no offices or even desk space inside, the streets in front of buildings were used. Only a few permits to use streets were granted at Wichita Falls, but the city of Burkburnett threw down the bars. Oil exchanges were opened on all of the streets in that city, where money for promoting oil companies was collected—and where leases and royalties were sold.

A street scene in Burkburnett during the boom was somewhat similar to that of a street fair or carnival. So common did the trading become in the exchanges that it was nothing unusual for a newly organized firm to have a drilling deal over-subscribed inside of a few hours. Often as high as forty-eight thousand dollars to ninety-eight thousand dollars would be collected in cash, inside a few hours, for a lease and drilling-well deal. Stock exchanges operated on a bigger scale in Wichita Falls and Fort Worth. Trading was active in Dallas, San Antonio, Amarillo, Denver, Oklahoma City, and other large cities—all dealing in Burkburnett oil properties.

Trading in these properties continued for nearly two years. However, the most active part of the boom was over in a little more than a year. Burkburnett's oil pool proper, the North-west Pool and the Red River bed producing area, covered a strip of land nine miles long and four miles wide, parallel with the river. This pool is about twelve miles north-east of the Electra oil-producing area.

In frontier life, Wichita Falls and Burkburnett rivalled California in the days of 1849. Dad's Corner, New Town, Bradley's Corner, and Bridge Town were filled with dance-hall girls, gamblers, bootleggers, and hi-jackers. Gay night life was as wild as that ever found in any frontier country. A number of men were murdered for their money during the heat of the boom. Bud Ballew, famous early-day officer at Ardmore, was killed at Wichita Falls by an officer of the law, toward the close.

Wichita Falls and Burkburnett both had open saloons at the beginning of the boom. National prohibition became effective about a year following the discovery of oil in the Fowler well. After the saloons were closed, bootlegging became the leading industry next to oil.

In my oil operations, I was in partnership with

J. B. Marlow, Mayor of Wichita Falls, and J. J. Perkins, a noted character and one of the wealthiest men in Texas. The firm's operations extended into territory including Cotton County, Oklahoma, where thousands of acres of leases were bought and sold. Marlow and I bid heavily for Comanche Indian lands, in Cotton County. As a result of our bidding, the price of lands auctioned off at Anardarko every three months increased from one dollar to as high as three hundred sixty-five dollars an acre. In every deal we paid off in cash. On one farm which we purchased at auction, we found upon examination of title that placer claims had been filed. This acted as a cloud on the title and prevented re-selling for a profit. A well was being drilled off-setting this tract of land. I had paid three hundred and sixty-five dollars an acre, and was in danger of losing in the event that the drilling well proved to be a duster. If a gusher, the lease could not have been sold because of bad title.

I made a hurried trip to Washington, hoping to get a refund of the money paid. This was my first trip since I resigned the marshalship. During my Government service I had been closely associated with John C. Koons, then a Postoffice Inspector. During the Woodrow Wilson Administration, Koons was an Assistant Postmaster General under Burleson. Koons, being an old friend, started to help me out after I had asked for assistance. He arranged for an interview with Cato Sells, Commissioner of Indian Affairs. We met Sells, and arranged a second meeting for ten o'clock the following forenoon. I did not take a lawyer along with me; but a high-powered attorney representing the Comanche tribe appeared before the Commissioner's Court, which was to decide about the proposed refund of money.

This attorney made a tearful plea—that made me want to cry—as he told of the poor Indian orphan whose land I had leased. I felt pretty small as I stood there listening to that powerful attorney, especially when I realized that I must plead my own case before that crowd. But when this attorney began to talk about orphans, I thought of the little motherless ones I had left at home in order to come to Washington and fight for our rights.

This orphan plea left me in anything but a good humor. I arose and told my story to the Court in plain, cowboy language—as truthfully as I knew how to talk. I told that Court, in reply to the Indian attorney, that when I had been United States Marshal under President Roosevelt, I took the same sacred oath which all officials in the Court had taken—the same oath the Indian attorney was making a lot of fuss about.

I explained to the Court that my babies were just as much Americans as the Comanche papoose; that I happened to know this Indian baby owned three quarter-sections of the richest land in Comanche County besides the quarter for which I had paid three hundred and sixty-five dollars an acre for just the oil and gas lease; and that the Government had been unable to give title to the land.

I talked for about an hour, when the Court asked me to place my statement in writing, which I did. On the following morning I appeared at the Department and received a refund check totaling $56,890. All of the purchase price was refunded except about $10,000.

Returning to Wichita Falls, I decided that, owing to the enormously congested living conditions, an oil town was a poor place to rear my children; so Kittie Joe, Vera Golda, Louie Van, Johnnie Martin, Temple Reeves, Pearlie, and Lucile all were placed in a boarding school.

In addition to supporting my own children, I now set aside a fund to provide for the support and education of thirteen orphans. These children were of good parentage, most of them being from Wichita Falls and Frederick. One young man, who wanted to become a minister of the Gospel, finished his education and was ordained. He is now pastor of a church in Texas.

I realized that I had a very heavy obligation if I was to keep up supporting the large number of children I had undertaken to look after. I decided to become a wildcatter on a big scale.

Colonel Albert E. Humphrey had just opened the great Mexia gusher oil pool in Limestone County, Texas. He was a wildcatter who later sold out for sixteen millions at Mexia. All of the country around Mexia was receiving a big oil play.

Freestone County, adjoining Limestone on the east, had a wonderful oil and gas structure. I took up a block of acreage making a location six miles south of the town of Teague, the county seat. The hole was drilled on the Gilham farm; the total depth being more than five thousand feet. This was one of the deepest tests in Texas in those days, and it proved to be a duster. The cost of this wildcat totaled $104,000, and all of the loss was paid by me. I did not sell an acre of the block to anybody, taking all of the gamble myself.

CHAPTER XXVII

LATER WOLF HUNTS

After I became interested in the oil business, the time sped by so rapidly that I could scarcely realize that years had passed since I had tried my hand at catching a live wolf. My wolf-catching exploits were often mentioned to me by people who had known me; but my business so engrossed my time and attention that it seemed impossible ever to find time for another hunt.

However, early in April, 1921, Will Ferguson, President of the Wichita Falls State Bank, with a small party of bankers and business men, including District Judge Ed Napier, all of Wichita Falls, planned for a wolf hunt in north-western New Mexico. Securing a pack of greyhounds before leaving Wichita Falls, they went by rail to Clayton, New Mexico, while I made the trip in an automobile, my son Temple accompanying me. The hunt was to be on Ferguson's ranch, some twenty-five or thirty miles west of Clayton. We were to be furnished horses for the chase after arriving at the ranch.

We arrived at the Ferguson Ranch in the middle of the day. We made our first chase that afternoon, but did not succeed in catching a wolf. The horses from the ranch were sufficiently speedy, but the difference between the altitude at Wichita Falls and that at the ranch (which was nearly seven thousand feet above sea level) was so great that the dogs were utterly unable to keep up with the wolves, much less to overtake them. We had another chase the next morning, and again the wolves outdistanced the greyhounds. The hunt had to be given up, the members of the party returning to their homes at Wichita Falls, Temple returning with them.

On our way back to Amarillo, Sheriff Roach told me that he would find a wolf that could be caught, and dogs that would have the speed to overtake and stop them. Accordingly, after arriving at Amarillo, the sheriff took his car, secured three good dogs, and, in company with the under-sheriff of his office, took me to his own ranch about thirty miles to the west.

When we arrived at the field, where we began to look for the wolves, we saw a bunch of antelopes. The sheriff took after a big buck prong-horn, running over the level buffalo grass sod. Sheriff Roach was a good driver, and when he turned his big Buick loose in the chase of that buck antelope, he made about forty miles an hour. The antelope was seldom more than a rod and a half ahead of us and slightly to one side. As the formation of an antelope is such that he can look backward as well as forward while running, he could see every move that we made. I stepped out on the running board, holding on to the windshield, with the intention of jumping on the antelope's back and grasping him by the horns if we could get close enough.

Although buffalo grass turf is not exactly smooth, the car made good speed except when leading to water, when there would be a very noticeable jolt. It so happened that the pit-cock which drains the water from the radiator tank was slightly loose, and it turned enough to let all of the water escape; whereupon the engine quickly heated to a point where it stopped so quickly that I was thrown over onto the hood of the engine. Of course, the antelope made good his escape.

We made our way slowly to the next tank, fed by a windmill pump, and refilled the radiator. Within two or three miles after starting off again, we discovered a big wolf going down a long sloping divide near the Canadian River. He was nearly two miles away when first sighted, going at right angles to the course we were going. Slightly changing our course, Sheriff Roach planned to meet the wolf before it could get on to lower and rougher ground. The wolf was still a half-mile away from us when the dogs were released. The car outran them until it overtook the wolf, running parallel with it until the dogs caught up. I jumped from the running board, took a hand in the fray, and caught the wolf.

This was the first time I had ever caught a wolf from an automobile. This wolf was brindled in color, brown with narrow black stripes. I gave him to the sheriff and understand he was on exhibition in Amarillo for some weeks.

Seven years after these two hunts in New Mexico and the Texas Panhandle—in April, 1928—I was in Fort Worth for a time. While there, some of my friends drew me into reminiscences concerning some of my experiences in coursing wolves and capturing them alive. It was while I was talking with two of my friends, both of whom were prominent jurists in the State Courts of Dallas—Judges H. S. Lattimore and R. H. Buck—that it was suggested that an old-time wolf hunt be arranged in the near future.

As this hunt was planned, it was to be staged on the ranch of Mr. Fred Foreman, a few miles northeast of Throckmorton, the county seat of Throckmorton County, about one hundred and fifty miles to the westward and slightly south of Fort Worth. The lands of that section were more or less rough, broken, and rolling, with timbered areas and prairies interspersed in about equal proportions—a good country for wolves but not the best terrain for catching them. Horses and hounds were to be furnished locally. Indeed, all of the saddle animals were to be supplied from Mr. Foreman's ranch.

In the party from Fort Worth, besides Judges Lattimore, Buck, and myself, were my son Temple and young R. E. McCarty, son of Mrs. Lillie McCarty, to whom I was married several months later.

We drove to the ranch during the afternoon of the day before the hunt. We were all astir very early the next morning, and were in the saddle at daybreak. When we were ready to start, our party had been increased by the arrival of the following local huntsmen: Gee Parrott, Thomas Boyd, John Bell, Rife Carpenter, Doctor Johnson, and Homer Moore, with our host, Fred Foreman, of course; also Doctor Harold and William Darden, who furnished the greyhounds for the occasion.

Apparently the ranges of the Foreman ranch furnished ideal conditions for timber wolves, which were known to be fairly numerous in that section. But we scoured various portions of the ranch during the forenoon without routing out a single lobo. The day proved to be a warm one, so that by noon all horses and riders were tired.

In the afternoon it was decided to resort to automobiles instead of taking to the saddle animals again. This afforded an additional advantage in that it kept the greyhounds fresh and ready for a chase. They rode in the cars instead of following after the horses, hot and panting in the afternoon sun.

Having worked over much of the Foreman ranch in the forenoon, we crossed to the ranges of the Hashknife ranch in the afternoon. There, quite unexpectedly, we came upon three wolves, grouped together in an open prairie glade. Evidently unalarmed, these wolves stood and looked at us very intently. At my suggestion, the driver of the car in which I was riding began to make a circuit of the glade, driving entirely around the wolves, which still kept watching us as if puzzled at our manoeuvers. Still continuing the encircling drive and gradually narrowing the distance between the car and the wolves, we finally approached within fifty paces of the animals without their showing the slightest alarm or panic. Then I suddenly jumped from the car, at the same time shouting to the man in another car to turn the greyhounds loose.

As I ran directly toward the three wolves, two of them fled in the opposite direction, toward the nearest timber. Without shifting its position, the other continued to stand facing me, so intently interested in my movements, and apparently so unafraid, that it did not notice the approach of the hounds from another quarter until they were almost upon him and ready to attack.

In the meantime, I was making the best speed of which I was capable. When the greyhounds tackled the wolf, it was too late for it to seek safety in flight. Instantly there was a furious struggle between the lobo and the hounds, in the course of which the now thoroughly enraged animal nearly severed the tongue of one of the latter.

It was at this stage of the fight that I reached the scene of the combat, out of breath as the result of the short run at a spurt of speed to which I had long been unaccustomed. Just as I arrived, the powerful beast threw off the greyhounds—which had gathered fresh courage as the result of such reinforcement—and the wolf then sprang at me. Warding off this charge, I gave it my right hand—as I had been wont to do in similar contests in the days of from twenty to thirty-five years before—and soon I had the satisfaction of holding the vicious animal securely by the lower jaw.

It was an excited and hilariously joyous crowd that came rushing toward me from the cars then, for none of them had ever seen such a feat performed before.

The wolf's jaws were bloody from the wound which it had inflicted on the tongue of an attacking greyhound; and, of course, some of this blood showed on my hand. Thereupon anxious inquiries were made as to whether I had been bitten. To this I answered, "No," adding, however, that I believed the jaws of a live wolf could pinch a little harder than they could twenty-five years ago!

The captive lobo was taken to Throckmorton, where it was presented alive to the municipality. A substantial cage was furnished for it, where it was still living when I inquired about it, several months later.

The capture of this wolf did not end the hunt, however; for, after the evening meal, all of the members of the hunting party took to the saddles again and, this time with trail hounds, the hunt was resumed. These trail hounds were furnished by Doctor Johnson and Messrs. Parrott, Carpenter, Homer Moore, and Sam Ridley. The whole of the night was spent in running wolves to the accompaniment of the musical baying of the hound pack. To be sure, no wolves were captured or killed (since it calls for action rather than advance advertising to land a lobo), but it was thrilling and exciting sport, just the same. The horses, hounds, and men were all tired and hungry when morning came, especially the men, for they had been at it for twenty-four hours. The Fort Worth contingent of the hunting party drove home that morning after breakfast.

Such, in brief, is the story of my last wolf hunt.

Sometimes I like to live over in retrospect some of those exciting and adventurous scenes of my earlier life, and then I wonder if it shall ever be my privilege to take part again in another wolf hunt. Although big timber wolves and vicious lobos are not nearly so numerous as they were in those days, they are not uncommon in some localities even to this day. And although I may have lost some of my agility with the flight of the years, I can scarcely believe that my right hand has lost its cunning or that I should be lacking in skill, physical strength, or mental alertness to prove, should occasion arise, that man still holds dominion over the beasts of the field.

CHAPTER XXVIII

FACE TO FACE WITH DEATH

Greater oil fields were being located and developed in various sections of the oil country. Wildcatters were looking toward Central Texas—the land of the old-time cattle ranges—as the coming country of the major oil development. The lure of both fame and fortune in wildcatting again appealed to me, and I secured a block of sixteen hundred acres of oil and gas leases in Bastrop County, Texas, in the spring of 1929. This district at that time was in a strictly wildcat area. In later days, a producing oil field was opened only a short distance from the Abernathy acreage block.

I staked a wildcat location on the Moore farm, twelve miles west of the town of Bastrop, the county seat. This well is twenty-nine miles east of the city of Austin. Before staking the Moore No. 1, I had completed four other wells in this same area. Although I had failed to get producers, I picked up excellent oil showings up in each of the four, and I was determined to find the rich pay-oil sand which I believed existed in that area. In drilling the Moore No. 1, I picked up a rich pay sand showing oil, below two thousand eight hundred feet. The Moore No. 1 well was drilled during the summer of 1930—a few months before the completion of the Discovery well in Henderson County, also before the sensational development in Gregg and other counties of East Texas.

218

About a year before, taking up the wildcat block in Bastrop County, I had met Mrs. Lillie McCarty, a widow, at Gainesville, Texas. She was the mother of two sons—R. E. and Monroe McCarty. I married Mrs. McCarty, the ceremony being performed by the Reverend Mr. McClung, in the First Baptist Church at Denton, Texas, August 29, 1928, and once more had a home of my own.

I needed that comfort, for I was now to be called upon to go through some of the most severe and distressing experiences of my life.

The depression hit me very hard and I lost nearly all the money I had previously accumulated. Because of my impoverished condition, I was obliged to discharge all my help on the well except a one-legged fireman, Roy Martin. I kept Martin because he had a family to support. I was running the rig myself to save expenses. The Moore No. 1, on which I was at work, was cased below twenty-three hundred feet, the total depth of the hole being more than twenty-eight hundred feet. The drill had gone into a pay-oil sand, a total of about eleven feet, and the hole was standing full of oil and water. This well, as nearly as I can estimate, was making about eight barrels of oil, with one hundred barrels of water, a day. By running the swab, I believed it possible to exhaust the water and increase the flow of oil.

On August 12, 1930, I made several runs with the swab, lowering the fluid to the bottom of the casing. The well was showing more oil—doing much better than during the previous day of swabbing. About nine-thirty that morning I sent the swab down into the well. I had a heavy feeling in my heart when I went to work that day, feeling that something would happen.

I applied the power and the swab started to lift its load of fluid from the bottom. When the line tightened I realized that the load was a heavy one and I looked at the boilers and noticed there were two hundred and ten pounds of steam on each pot.

Suddenly Jim Robertson, a cable driller who had been watching me, called out,

"You'll never get out; you have too big a load!"

"Stand back from the derrick, Jim! Something might happen!" I shouted.

I was standing with both feet inside the lever, with my left hand on the throttle, giving the engine every ounce of steam it would take, when the line snapped after the swab had been pulled about fifty feet. (The cable was of five-eighths-inch steel wire.)

Racing at its highest speed, the engine started running away with itself, threatening to wreck the machinery. There was no load and all of the high-pressure steam was going into the engine. Only about one hundred and fifty feet of the wire line remained on the drum when the cable snapped, and, like a wild coiling snake, it wrapped itself around my waist, jerking me into the drum.

Quick as a flash, Roy Martin, whom I previously had told to remain at the engine, shut off the power. Had he not been right on the job, my body would have been torn to pieces or cut in two. From the time I heard the crash and felt the fearful coil of that cable around my body I felt I was a goner.

It took Jim Robertson and Roy Martin thirty minutes to unwind the wire cable, which had burned its way through my flesh to the bone, crushing my ribs.

I was given up for dead by those men, and to all appearances I was dead. My eyes were out of my head, my tongue protruded from my mouth, and I lay cold and motionless on the derrick floor for an hour and a half. During this time my body was burning up with a heat I cannot describe. It seemed like the fires of hell itself.

Roy Martin drove my car five miles to the town of Cedar Creek, whence he called Mrs. Abernathy, at Austin, telling her:

"Your husband was killed instantly on the derrick floor." Martin then called the morgue in Austin, twenty-nine miles distant, asking that the dead wagon be sent. He then called for a doctor at Bastrop to come and make an examination of the body and certify as to the cause of death.

The doctor upon arrival pronounced me dead. My body was then loaded into the dead wagon, and the driver started for Austin. Although I could not move, I realized that I was inside something which was moving; and, when the driver stopped on the road, I plainly heard the voice of some one ask,

"Oh! is he really dead?" and the answer of the driver, "Yes."

The inquirer was my wife, who had arrived on the scene. She sprang at once into the dead wagon and I felt her warm hand as it touched my brow. I would have given everything had she kept it there— but she could not stand that cold feeling of death and quickly withdrew it. At the time they pronounced me dead, at the well, the doctor had said that my heart action had stopped. Mrs. Abernathy, however, noticed that I was still breathing, although very faintly, and she excitedly declared to Mr. Starkey, who had accompanied her from Austin:

"Oh! Mr. Starkey, he is *not* dead! He is breathing. Driver, take him to the best hospital in Austin."

On the way to the hospital I began to crave water. I wanted something cool on my parched tongue. Mrs. Abernathy must have noticed it, for she asked the driver to stop at the next house. But when she gave me a teaspoonful of water, I strangled, and she cried:

"Oh, I am afraid I have killed him!"

When they arrived with my body at the emergency hospital, Dr. Brownlee, in response to the pleading of Mrs. Abernathy, directed that I should be taken to the big hospital at Austin, telling Mrs. Abernathy he would get Dr. Scott to meet him there.

They thought I was unconscious when they took me into the hospital, but I knew and could hear all that was going on around me. I heard Doctor Scott say:

"His ribs are crushed! What will we do with those eyes? I am afraid, should he live, that he will be blind!" And, indeed, I was blind for some time thereafter.

My son Temple was head driller on a core test outfit for the Humble Oil Co., near San Antonio. On the day of the accident, the driller employed on another shift came to the core test well and asked:

"What relation are you to Jack Abernathy?"

"He's my father," was Temple's reply.

"He's dead! He was killed instantly near Austin, I saw by the paper in San Antonio today."

Leaving the job immediately, Temple came to

Austin, to the emergency hospital, but he was informed that his father had been taken to another hospital.

When Temple was permitted to see me, he said to Mrs. Abernathy,

"He will never live. I have seen too many oilfield accidents. I am going to get a leave of absence and come here to stay."

"You have a big family to support, and you had better stay with your job. I will not leave his bedside," was Mrs. Abernathy's reply.

A few hours later, however, Temple came back to Austin in order to remain with me. I could hear everything that Temple said to Mrs. Abernathy as they discussed the case. On the second day, Jim Robertson and Roy Martin were permitted to enter the room. When I realized they were present, I scribbled on a piece of paper:

"Ask Jim Robertson if my body ever moved."

Mrs. Abernathy says that Jim and Roy stood there with their arms folded, gazing at me. When she read the writing on the slip to Jim, I heard him say:

"Dead men never move. Had he ever moved, it would have scared me to death!"

He could not be convinced that I was not actually dead when I lay on the derrick floor.

Jim and Roy were two good and faithful men, and I knew they liked me. The two doctors cared for me with the greatest devotion. The two nurses were excellent. But my dear wife, who sat there night and day, would not leave my bedside. I want to praise her to the world for her kind and devoted attention during my whole sickness.

When I began to show signs of steady improvement, I was removed from the hospital to my home in Austin, where I could lie on a glassed-in porch. The doctors attended me from two to three times a day, and about three months after the accident I began to see again, although my eyes were badly crossed. I had about given up all hope of ever again being a well man. The injuries in my back from the wire coils refused to show signs of healing.

I now heard of the Rev. H. B. Taylor, San Antonio, who was preaching the doctrine of divine healing. Believing that he could help me, as soon as I was able I went to San Antonio and attended Dr. Taylor's meetings for over a week. The good Doctor prayed with me and for me, and I prayed most fervently for myself. Soon my eyes became straightened so I could see with them as well as ever; the injuries in my back began to heal; and I returned to my family, feeling that I was on the road to recovery.

Whatever the reader may think, I believe that my prayers were answered. At any rate, I am setting down the exact facts of this great experience in my life, for they are a part of the record and have wrought a marvellous change in my thought and life.

FINIS